AUSTRIAN IMMIGRATION TO CANADA

AUSTRIAN IMMIGRATION TO CANADA
SELECTED ESSAYS

*Edited by*
*Franz A.J. Szabo*

Carleton University Press

Printed and bound in Canada

---

**Canadian Cataloguing in Publication Data**

Main entry under title:
    Austrian immigration to Canada : selected essays

Essays originally presented at a symposium on Austrian
    immigration in Canada held at Carleton University,
    Ottawa, in May 1995.
Companion vol. to a History of Austrian migration to
    Canada.
Includes bibliographical references.
ISBN 0-88629-281-6

1. Austrian Canadians—History. I. Szabo,
Franz A. J.

| FC106.A9A98 1996 | 971'.00436 | C96-900280-7 |
| F1035.A9A98 1996 | | |

---

Cover Design: Your Aunt Nellie
Typeset: Mayhew & Associates/Chisholm Communications, Ottawa, Ontario

Carleton University Press gratefully acknowledges the support extended to its
publishing program by the Canada Council and the financial assistance of the
Ontario Arts Council. The Press would also like to thank the Department of
Canadian Heritage, Government of Canada, and the Government of Ontario
through the Ministry of Culture, Tourism and Recreation, for their assistance.

# CONTENTS

Acknowledgements                                                      vii

Introduction
    The Austrian Immigrant and the
    Canadian Multicultural Spectrum
    *Franz A.J. Szabo*                                                  1

I     German-Speaking Immigrants of Many Backgrounds
     and the 1990s Canadian Identity
     *Dirk Hoerder*                                                    11

II    Demographic Patterns of Austrian Canadians, 1900-1991
     *Gertrud Neuwirth and John de Vries*                              33

III   Push and Pull Factors for Overseas Migrants from Austria-
     Hungary in the 19th and 20th Centuries
     *Michael John*                                                    55

IV   Austrians Abroad: Austrian Emigration after 1945
     *Traude Horvath and Gerda Neyer*                                  83

V     The Largest Austrian Dialect Speech-Island in North America
     *Herfried Scheer*                                                 93

VI   The Trudeau-Kreisky Connection:
     Austria and Canada on the Road to Cancún
     *Oliver Rathkolb*                                                103

VII  The Empire Replanted: The Enrichment of Canada's Musical
     Life by Austrian Immigrants in the 20th Century
     *Paul McIntyre*                                                  113

VIII The History of the Egger Family of Immigrants to Canada
     *Thomas Samhaber*                                                127

IX   Immigration: A Personal Retrospective of an Austrian
     in Canada
     *Helmut Walter Ott*                                              135

## ACKNOWLEDGEMENTS

Production of this volume would not have been possible without the generous financial support of government agencies both in Canada and in Austria. In the first instance we owe our special gratitude to the Government of Canada's Secretary of State for Multiculturalism and the Status of Women, Department of Canadian Heritage, for helping to subsidize our symposium on Austrian immigration to Canada, and making it possible to invite scholars and members of the community from across Canada and from Europe. Particular thanks are due to the officials in the Heritage department who expedited our conference grant request, Mark Curfoot-Mollington and Susanne Samson. Secondly, we owe an incalculable debt of gratitude to the Austrian ambassador to Canada, His Excellency, Dr. Walther G. Lichem, who not only took time to attend our conference, but at whose personal initiative a publication subsidy for this volume was secured from the Austrian Federal Ministry for External Affairs (Bundesministerium für auswärtige Angelegenheiten). We thank the Ministry for its generous support. We are also grateful to G. Struart Adam, Dean of the Faculty of Arts of Carleton University, for the additional support he gave the conference, to John Flood, general editor of Carleton University Press, for taking on this publication project at short notice, and to Jennie Strickland, our copy editor, for saving us from a multitude of technical errors.

# INTRODUCTION
## THE AUSTRIAN IMMIGRANT AND THE CANADIAN
## MULTICULTURAL SPECTRUM

*Franz A.J. Szabo*
*Carleton University*


THE IMMIGRANT IS FATED to be a Janus-faced creature. The condition is a familiar one to many generations of newcomers to Canada—never completely at home in the adopted country, nonetheless increasingly out of touch with the realities of the country of origin. Many of them report the sense of alienation that comes from being "at home nowhere," except perhaps on board the aircraft which transports them between the two lands. It is because of such duality that it will perhaps come as no surprise that the impetus for a systematic study of the Austrian immigration to Canada should have come from an anniversary in Austrian history. On 1 November 1996 a famous central European medieval document will be a thousand years old. That document marks the first recorded use of the word *Ostarrîchi*, medieval forerunner of the modern German, *Österreich* —that is, Austria.[1] The approach of that date and the ensuing "millennium" celebrations in Austria, and among Austrians throughout the world, inspired a group of Canadian and Austrian scholars to take up the little studied subject of the Austrian migration to Canada.

The results of this collaborative research effort have been published under the title *A History of the Austrian Migration to Canada*.[2] The genesis, objectives and development of the project that resulted in this book are described in detail in the preface to that volume, but a central part of the research project was the convening of an international symposium, both to act as a traditional academic forum to vet research findings, but also to give Austrian immigrants from all over Canada an opportunity to react to and comment on research of which they themselves had been the subjects. It was, at first, our intention to present the eleven papers of the originally assembled research team at this symposium, but while this research was being conducted, a call for additional papers went out to the scholarly community both in North America and in Austria. By the time the conference was held at Carleton University in May 1995, this call had yielded such a positive response that the number of papers offered for presentation at the conference had risen to twenty-five. Since the original research project had set about to produce a systematic survey of the Austrian migration to Canada rather than to present a random selection of conference papers, most of the additional papers that were offered for the conference could not fit with the parameters of the volume we were planning to publish. As a result, plans were made to bring out this supplementary volume, which presents a selection from the other papers presented at the Austrian Immigration to Canada symposium. Those papers fell into three broad categories: traditional academic research papers, shorter research notes on ancillary aspects of the main theme, and reports, family histories and memoirs of the Austrian immigrants themselves. This compilation presents a selection from each of these categories.

The first three essays are traditional academic research papers. In the first, Dirk Hoerder challenges the conventional pieties of the label "German-Canadians"—under which Austrian migrants are usually subsumed. His essay shows that the assertion of a collective German-Canadian identity, and the assumption of homogeneity within that putative linguistic group group "has only limited factual basis." The second paper, a collaborative effort by Gertrud Neuwirth and John de Vries, is devoted to a close analysis of Canadian immigration and census statistics in the twentieth century, and shows how these data "give an inflated picture" of the actual number of Austrians who have migrated to and are currently living in Canada. The third essay by Michael John attempts to come to grips with the complexities of emigration out of the old Austro-Hungarian Empire. He shows that significant emigration from the Dual Monarchy only began in the 1890s, and that in this major pre-World War I migration wave "the German-speaking population was strongly underrepresented."

The second group of papers are shorter research notes. Traude Horvath and Gerda Neyer briefly report on a major project of the Austrian Academy of Sciences devoted to the problem of Austrian emigration throughout the world. The linguist, Herfried Scheer, shows how an Austrian dialect idiom migrated with religious dissenters through Europe, and eventually arrived in Canada to build the largest Austrian dialect speech island in North America. Oliver Rathkolb reports on the common global activities of Austria and Canada under their respective Prime Ministers, Bruno Kreisky and Pierre Elliott Trudeau. Our troika in the memoirs category opens with the composer Paul McInytre's account of the influence of Austrian immigrants on Canada's musical life. Thomas Samhaber recounts the migratory saga of his great-grandparents as reflected in family letters preserved by him. Finally Helmut Walter Ott presents a personal memoir of his own childhood immigration experience. These papers do not exhaust all the presentations at the Austrian Immigration to Canada conference. Some appear in a revised form in the main volume, while others were short reports from Austrian communities across Canada which were not suitable for publication. On the whole, however, it is hoped that a beginning has been made in detailing the Austrian migration to Canada and in describing some of the specific experiences of Austrian immigrants. This may represent only a very small chapter of Canadian history, but it is nevertheless one without which the broader picture of immigration to this country cannot be complete.

In a recent study of the Italian immigration experience to Canada, one of this country's most important historians in the field of ethnic history, Roberto Perin, pointed out with what "lack of concern and compassion" traditional Canadian historiography had long viewed the peculiar experiences of the immigrants to this country. Only in the last few decades have these historians begun to integrate the realities of the migrants' experiences and the various accommodations immigrants have had to make in order to "get by" into the larger fabric of Canadian history.[3] As Canadian historians gradually come to realize that a fuller and more sophisticated understanding of the immigration experience is central to any balanced comprehension of Canadian history and society, the need for detailed micro-histories of the various dimensions of this experience is obvious. Such histories, however, present numerous difficulties. Often motivated by filio-pietistic and political impulses, they have a tendency to maximize the size, cohesiveness and importance of an ethnic group, with the intent of staking a claim in the highly politicized terrain of multiculturalism and conflicting conceptions of Canadian society. On the historiographical level, there is also the theoretical problem of how to integrate such studies into Canadian history, since these involve the extremely delicate issues of identity and cultural retention and transmission, as well as the methodologically even more challenging question of the manner and degree to which the receiving society is transformed by immigrants.

One of the prime objectives of publishing the Austrian immigration research project findings, as well as this companion volume, is to help locate and define the place of the Austrians in the Canadian multicultural spectrum with more clarity and precision. This immediately raises a number of very complex questions on the Austrian identity and its place within any broader German-Canadian linguistic grouping. There are two quite distinct hermeneutic dynamics at work here: on the one hand, there is the essentially European problem of the relationship between German language and ethnicity; on the other hand, there is the particular Canadian problem of ethnic group status within the "Canadian Family Tree"[4] with its inherent tendency to maximize demographic claims. With respect to the first of these problems, any effort to posit an all-inclusive pan-German ethnicity necessarily labours under the shadows of the Nazi past. In the Canadian context, on the other hand, pan-German fusions give demographic weight to the claim that "they, too, founded Canada."[5] In this regard, our two volumes on the Austrian immigration to Canada might seem thoroughly counter-productive to the enterprise of claim-staking. By asserting, as we do, that Austrians constitute a distinct ethnicity we implicitly diminish the "German-Canadian" presence in this country. What is more, our studies do not even try to maximize the number of Austrians, and if anything they reveal that those numbers are smaller than official statistics might lead one to conclude. What our findings suggest, however, is that no Canadian analysis of the problem can divorce itself from the European framework from which it originated, no matter how convenient such isolation might be.

English, Spanish or French conceptions of a broader linguistic unity within an "English-speaking world," a Hispanic linguistic community or a "Francophonie" impute little sense of pan-linguistic nationhood. Notions of distinct nations within a broader "Germanophonie,"[6] on the other hand, have laboured in a hothouse of competing conceptions of *"Deutschtum"* and *"Kulturnation."* The literal translations of these terms —"Germanness" and "Cultural Nation" respectively—do not even begin to touch on the many subtle nuances of the German words. The notion of *Deutschtum*, rooted in the philosophy of Johann Gottfried Herder, was central to the *völkish* ideology of the Nazi movement, and though it is important to stress that not all adherents of the concept of *Deutschtum* were Nazis, the sense of pan-German ethnicity remains its central premise. Closely related to this is the notion, already well articulated by

Friedrich Schiller, that though the Germans were politically divided into many states, they constituted a single nation in the cultural sense. This second concept of Germans as a *Kulturnation* was burdened by fewer of the racial implications contained in the notion of *Deutschtum*, but its premise, too, posited a single ethnicity, and, as Jürgen Kocka pointed out, has pan-German implications in its contemporary usage.[7] Although both notions seem to have suffered irretrievable losses in the public discourse of the European arena, the full implications of the debate do not always seem to be clear to proponents of a single "German-Canadian" identity in this country. Part of the problem is that the latter often seem insufficiently informed about these larger debates. Another part of the problem is that the literature on German language groups in Canada is relatively slight,[8] and that the major work on the subject is a translation of pre-World War II works of Heinz Lehmann[9]—an historian heavily anchored in concepts of *Deutschtum*. Also of importance, no doubt, is the fact that a pan-German linguistic reckoning gives "German-Canadians" claim to the third largest language group in this country.

This brings us directly to the second problem of the integration of "ethnic history" and the immigrant experience into the broader stream of Canadian history. If Canadian historians have gradually transformed the immigrant from "outcast" to "actor"—that is, from passive subject to active protagonist in Canadian history,[10] the concomitant prerequisite obviously has to be a clearer understanding of immigrant identities. That immigrants would become active agents of Canadian history became apparent with the establishment in 1963 of the Royal Commission on Bilingualism and Biculturalism. Already in their preliminary report of 1965, the commissioners, focused as they were on the "crisis" in the relationship between the "two founding nations," were disconcerted to discover the degree of dissent against the "dual nature" of Canada theory which emerged under the conceptual umbrella of "multiculturalism." Latent fears about "Balkanization" clearly mark the report, and the commissioners went out of their way to attempt to marginalize this dissent by suggesting that the proponents of such views proceeded from "an overestimation of their numbers." The commissioners themselves, by using narrowly circumscribed "mother tongue" statistics from the census of 1961 to assign identities, were able to persuade themselves that, in "proper perspective," Canada was essentially bicultural, and that all the "others" put together (including all aboriginal peoples) constituted just under 14 percent of the total population.[11]

By the time the various volumes of the final report began to appear from 1967 onward, the victory of the "others" over the Davidson Dunton/Laurendeau commission was evident, as the commissioners were now forced to admit:

In both absolute figures and percentages, the part of the population neither British nor French in origin has continued to increase. While the total Canadian population more than quadrupled between 1881 and 1961, the number of people of other extractions multiplied tenfold.... If immigration and emigration continue in the patterns that have prevailed in Canada since World War I, it is possible that the total number of people of other ethnic origins could in the not-distant future surpass both the number of those of French origin and those of British origin.[12]

Though the efforts of commissioner Jaroslav Rudnyckyj—expressed in his "separate statement"—to have German, Ukrainian and Italian recognized as unofficial regional languages of Canada came to little, his theoretical division of the languages of Canada into three categories—indigenous, colonial and immigrant—did begin to point to the more pluralistic conceptions of culture that were to emerge in the 1970s.[13] Soon, "biculturalism" gave way to "multiculturalism" and this new concept quickly received legislative enshrinement in the Canadian Multiculturalism Act which followed. This legislation gave spokesmen of various ethnic groups an opportunity to stake claim to what Robert Harney called "auxiliary founding people" status[14]—particularly when grants and subsidies were to be had in the process. The image of the "cultural mosaic" became ever more common in the debates, as each group sought to find its place on the ethnic spectrum.

At stake in this debate was the whole question of the immigrant's identity—a question which we tend to see in slightly different terms now than multicultural advocates did in the 1970s. Much recent scholarship on ethnic identity has been influenced by such analysts as Benedict Anderson and Eric Hobsbawn, who have conceived of "nations" as "imagined communities," and who have emphasized the degree to which these are intellectual constructs rather than primordial realities.[15] As one of Canada's foremost experts on "nation-building," Paul Robert Magocsi has pointed out, the normal state of affairs for most people is a "hierarchy of multiple loyalties" that encompass a broad range of social, occupational, confessional, familial, and regional dimensions.[16] Nor is an ethnic identity necessarily ascriptive or mutually exclusive, as emigrants from the old

Austro-Hungarian Empire demonstrated all too well. Efforts in the old imperial army to keep ethnic statistics, for example, often broke down when individual recruits who spoke two or more languages indiscriminately could not report a special consciousness of any particular nationality.[17] In a multi-ethnic states such as the Habsburg Monarchy—and Canada for that matter—where children are quite frequently the products of inter-ethnic marriage, it is quite natural to find individuals who feel perfectly comfortable with one or more "national" loyalties. What is more, as social scientists have begun to argue, "situational or optional ethnicity," in which an individual's identification can be "consciously emphasized or de-emphasized as the situation requires," is quite widespread.[18] With nearly one third of the Canadian population taking advantage of the new "multiple origin" category in the census of 1991,[19] the scope for "situational ethnicity" is clearly great, and growing greater by the day.

Seen in this light, the immigrant is hardly the standard-bearer of an immutable old-word identity which he or she contributes as a fixed gem to the mosaic or kaleidoscope of Canadian multiculturalism. Much argument in favour of "heritage languages" and "cultural retention" is framed in these simplistic terms, and critics who attempt to debunk such efforts largely miss the central point. Identity is a complex problem and "cultural retention" somewhat of a straw horse. Immigrants come to this country with layers of identity, some of which are progressively shed while others are acquired. It is the degree of cultural transmission that occurs during this process that should be of primary interest, for the original dimensions of immigrant identity do not simply evaporate. Rather, they become part of the complex of cultural traditions that shape—often in transmuted ways—the Canadian social fabric. The resulting multicultural mix, however, does not depend on linguistic pluralism. Heritage languages can be valuable cultural assets to aid in broader cosmopolitan understanding, but if their cultivation attempts to preserve an ascriptive ethnic identity, it risks ghettoization and becomes thoroughly counter-productive. Such efforts seldom succeed over the long haul in any case, and are usually driven by external factors more than by any internal existential anxiety.

Language issues notwithstanding, it is important to remember that the immigrant *is* a product of a particular culture, and that that culture fundamentally affects the host society. Perhaps it would be more productive if we saw these immigrant cultures less in terms of language and ethnicity and more in terms of specific histories and cultural traditions, of habits of thought and patterns of creativity. The problem for the immigrant is that, while, in time he or she can easily acquire either or both of the official languages of Canadian society, an elemental relationship with the myths of Canadian history can never be expected. It is often remarked that an emigrant's perception of the old country is frozen in time at the moment of emigration; it is less frequently noted that the history of the new country only begins for the immigrant at the moment of immigration. Stephen Leacock's well-known, if condescending bon mot "Leave them alone and pretty soon the Ukrainians will think they won the battle of Trafalgar," is only true insofar as, left alone, Ukrainians will think Canada is their country as much as anyone else's, but what they will and can never think is that they won the battle of Trafalgar. The historical myths that shaped them involved Khmelnytsky and Mazepa, not Wolfe and Montcalm, cossacks not *coureurs-de-bois*, haidamaks not *patriotes*. But by this measure the historical roots of the immigrants are thus the historical roots of Canada as well, and Canadian historians who wish to develop a more balanced understanding of Canadian society must seek to understand these roots, as well as the dominant English and French ones which shaped institutions and structures.

A clear understanding of this problem is also necessary for a fuller analysis of the immigrant's impact on the receiving society. As early as the Report of the Royal Commission on Bilingualism and Biculturalism one could read such eloquent tributes as this:

Canadian culture has been the richer for the knowledge, skills, and traditions which all the immigrant groups brought with them. Their many distinctive styles of life have gradually increased the range of experience, outlook, ideas, and talents which characterize the country. Cultural diversity has widened our horizons; it has also given us opportunities— not always seized upon—for varied approaches to the solution of our problem.[20]

Thus, while it was and is widely conceded that the culture of the receiving society was altered by the arrival of immigrants, precisely how and where this has happened has remained largely undefined. Doubtless, however, one can never hope to assess the transformation of the society immigrants have wrought without a more sophisticated understanding of the cultures of which these immigrants were products. In as broad a multicultural spectrum as Canada's, this may be a daunting task, but it will increasingly become one of the great challenges of Canadian history to cultivate precisely such sensibilities. Our project is but a small contribution to this enterprise.

ENDNOTES

1.  The English word is borrowed from the Latin, but the Latin word "Austria" only
    came into common usage in the middle of the 12th century. On the *Ostarrîchi*
    document and related problems of nomenclature see Richard Müller, "Der Name
    Österreich," *Blätter des Vereins für Landeskunde Niederösterreichs* Neue Folge 35
    (1901), 402-38; Alphons Lhotsky, *Ostarrîchi* (Vienna, 1946); Leo Santifaller, *Über
    die Ostarrîchi-Urkunde vom 1. November 996* (Vienna, 1948); Karl Klimesch, *Zur
    Herkunft der Wörter "Österreich" und "Austria"* (Vienna, 1950); Erich Zöllner,
    "1000 Jahre Österreich: Die Babenberger und ihre Epoche," *Almanach der
    österreichischen Akademie der Wissenscahften* 126 (1976), 236-58.
2.  Frederick C. Engelmann, Manfred Prokop and Franz A.J. Szabo, eds., *A History of
    the Austrian Migration to Canada* (Ottawa, 1996).
3.  Roberto Perin, "The Immigrant: Actor or Outcast," in Roberto Perin and Franc
    Sturino, eds., *Arrangiarsi: The Italian Immigration Experience in Canada*
    (Montreal, 1989), pp. 10-12.
4.  The phrase is borrowed from successive editions of the Canadian Department of
    Citizenship and Immigration's *Notes on the Canadian Family Tree* (Ottawa, 1960
    et seq.).
5.  Rudolf A. Helling, *A Socio-Economic History of German-Canadians: They, too,
    Founded Canada* (Wiesbaden, 1984). See also Gerhard P. Bassler, "Silent or
    Silenced Co-Founders of Canada? Reflections on the History of German
    Canadians," *Canadian Ethnic Studies* 22 (1990), 38-46.
6.  For an excellent discussion of this problem, see Ignaz Seidl-Hohenveldern, "Die
    österreichische Nation in der Germanophonie," in Gottfried Ziegler, Boris
    Meissner and Dieter Blumenwitz, eds., *Deutschland als Ganzes: Rechtliche und
    Historische Überlegungen anläßlich des 70. Geburtstages von Herbert Czaja* (Cologne,
    1984), pp. 319-22.
7.  Jürgen Kocka, "Probleme der politischen Integration der Deutschen 1867 bis
    1945," in Otto Büsch and James J. Sheehan, eds., *Die Rolle der Nation in der
    deutschen Geschichte und Gegenwart* (Berlin, 1985), p. 118.
8.  Cf. Steven M. Benjamin, *The German-Canadians: A Working Bibliography*
    (Toronto, 1982), and most recently, Renée Rogers and Gabriele Scardellato, eds.,
    "Germans" in *A Bibliography of Canada's Peoples, 1980-1989* Vol. 2 (Toronto,
    1996), in press. I am indebted to Paul Robert Magocsi and the Multicultural
    History Society of Ontario for providing me with an advance copy of this forth-
    coming bibliography.
9.  Heinz Lehmann, *The German Canadians 1750-1937. Immigration, Settlement and
    Culture,* translated, edited and introduced by Gerhard P. Bassler from Lehmann's

*Zur Geschichte des Deutschtums in Kanada* (1931) and *Das Deutschtum in Westkanada* (1939)(St. John's, 1986).

10. Perin, "The Immigrant: Actor or Outcast," pp. 9-32.

11. A. Davidson Dunton, André Laurendeau, et als., *A Preliminary Report of the Royal Commission on Bilingualism and Biculturalism* (Ottawa, 1965), see especially pp. 50-53, 186-87. In a footnote (p. 50) the commissioners were forced to admit that ethnic identity as revealed by self-identification in the census yielded a figure almost twice as high.

12. A. Davidson Dunton, André Laurendeau, et al., *Report of the Royal Commission on Bilingualism and Biculturalism*, Vol. 1 (Ottawa, 1967), p. 22.

13. *Ibid.*, pp. 155-69.

14. Robert F. Harney, "Caboto and other *Parentela*: The Uses of the Italian-Canadian Past," in Perin and Sturino, *Arrangiarsi*, p. 40.

15. Benedict Anderson, *Imagined Communities: Reflections on the Origin and Spread of Nationalism* (London, 1983, 2nd ed., 1991); E.J. Hobsbawm, *Nations and Nationalism since 1780: Programme, Myth, Reality* (London, 1990, 2nd ed., 1992).

16. Paul Robert Magocsi, "The Ukrainian National Revival: A New Analytical Framework," *Canadian Review of Studies in Nationalism* 16 (1989), 50-52.

17. István Deák, *Beyond Nationalism: A Social and Political History of the Habsburg Officer Corps, 1848-1918* (New York, Oxford, 1990), p. 14.

18. Chew Sock Foon, "On the Incompatibility of Ethnic and National Loyalties: Reframing the Issue," *Canadian Review of Studies in Nationalism* 13 (1986), 1-11.

19. Statistics Canada, *Ethnic Origin* (Ottawa, 1993) [1991 Census of Canada], pp. 26-59, Table 1B.

20. *Report of the Royal Commission on Bilingualism and Biculturalism* I, xxv.

I

# GERMAN-SPEAKING IMMIGRANTS OF MANY
# BACKGROUNDS AND THE 1990S CANADIAN IDENTITY

## Dirk Hoerder
## University of Bremen

TWO GROUPS IN CANADA, the British and the French, have assigned themselves the role of "founding groups." All other immigrant groups have
summarily been called ethnics or allophones. Of the latter, the larger
groups, including the "Germans," have demanded official recognition of
their special role as co-founders. The work of the Royal Commission on
Bilingualism and Biculturalism from 1962 to 1968, and the policy of
multiculturalism since 1971 have led to a recognition of the role of the
"new Canadians" in the building of a Canadian culture, and a new level
of research into questions of immigration, acculturation and ethnic identity. The everyday practice of multicultural living has brought about
awareness of "multiple origins." Nevertheless, the recent debate about
multiculturalism, beginning with an immigrant writer's cry, of "don't call
me ethnic," suggests that a stock-taking is in order.[1]

This essay discusses, first, the relationship between group size and
political power, as well as social status. Why do groups, or some of their
members, have an interest in appearing to be a particularly large group?
Secondly, are ethnic groups in Canada as homogeneous as some of their
spokespersons argue? Thirdly, is it possible to reconstruct group sizes from
census data on immigration and ethnic identification? Fourthly, how do
today's Canadians define their identity—as ethnic or as Canadian?

### IDENTITY AND INTEREST

In scholarship and in politics it has been widely acknowledged—assimila-
tionist demands notwithstanding—that immigrant and refugee identities

change only slowly over time. Identity is understood as the whole inter-
nalized complex of norms, values—secular and spiritual—and customs
expressed in everyday living. It permits stability of personality; it prevents
individual breakdown or social anomie. Identity, as a social creation, also
permits self-determined changes by interaction with other members of
society: change from one stage in the life-cycle to the next or from immigrant to ethnic to dynamic, pluralist mainstream. Cultural identity can be
kept static only by special efforts, such as those of Mennonites and other
ethno-religious groups. Ongoing processes of acculturation, changing
from a pre- to a post-migration identity, can be interrupted by political
fiat and racist attitudes. Thus Japanese-Canadians during World War II
were forced into camps, into "secondary minority formation."

Since identities are largely socially constructed, their formation is
subject to specific in-group interests. Group leaders often have a vested
interest in group maintenance to keep their position; businessmen cater-
ing to ethnic needs try to keep their customers by preventing consump-
tion patterns from adjusting to mainstream society. Priests, journalists,
and other intellectuals can lose their clientele if the spiritual outlook, the
demand for news, and the construction of group histories and mentali-
ties no longer conform to old-world moulds. Group-based scholars may
support the particularist claims of their group in attempts to improve
their own positions either as gatekeepers or in the general scholarly
community.

Host-society interests influence the way in which ethnic groups are
viewed by Canadians. Group specifics may appear as an enrichment, as in
the policy of multiculturalism, or they may appear as cataclysmic, engulf-
ing "superior races" in amalgamation, as turn-of-the-century racists
argued when "Galicians" and "Orientals" began to arrive. Cultural diversity may be interpreted as divisive. Normative concepts of society are at
issue when individual rights and aspirations are juxtaposed to the aspirations of corporate groups, of ethnic cultures. Group identity can thus
appear as a haven for personal coherence of values and everyday practices,
as an interest-based tool used by elites to retain their position, as a culturally integrative whole, or as a repressive mechanism negating individual development. Given the internal diversity of many of the Canadian
ethnic groups, scholarly or political emphasis on the retention of an
assumedly singular and monocultural group identity may neither meet
the needs of the subgroups nor contribute to an adequate understanding
of acculturation.

## SCHOLARSHIP AND THE CONSTRUCTION OF IDENTITY: WHO ARE THE "GERMAN-CANADIANS"?

Recent scholarship has differentiated the "founding groups," from mono-cultural British and French groups to broadly conceived language groups, Anglophones and Francophones, and to ethno-cultural mosaics in themselves: the English, Scots, Welsh, and Irish and the Acadians, Québécois, Franco-Ontarians and French in each of the other provinces, as well as direct immigrants from France after 1763. Of the next largest groups, the Ukrainian-Canadians, who integrated culturally different East European newcomers,[2] became a political force in the 1960s, pressing for recognition of the New Canadians as contributors to a Canadian identity that was multifocal, rather than bipolar. The Italian-Canadian group, consisting of Northerners and Southerners of varying provincial origins, in the 1980s developed a sophisticated scholarly image of its social composition, gender roles, and acculturation processes.[3] The Yiddish-speaking group considered itself and was considered by parts of mainstream society a "third solitude."[4] Its internal differentiation was due to regionally diverse backgrounds and variations in religious practices. In all of these cases differentiated approaches to culture are a *conditio sine qua non* for sophisticated analyses. The German-language group attracted scholarly attention into the 1930s but thereafter was neglected. If we take its diversity into account, we can discuss inaccuracies and interests in self-perception and suggest some empirically sound approaches to "internal multiculturalism."

A recent historiographical essay on German-Canadians asserted that the group is one of the "co-founders of Canada," but became a "silenced as well as the silent" group. Another study is subtitled "They, too, founded Canada."[5] Both authors agree that the German-Canadians have "received scant attention." Other historians have looked in vain for German-Canadian contributions; e.g., to the labor movement, where German-Americans played a major role.[6] An exhaustive bibliography of "German Canadiana" lists a wealth of publications but no major recent studies that meet social science history standards.[7] No scholar has yet produced a survey in the popular "Generations Series." Lehmann's study from the 1930s, sensitively revised by Bassler, has been the only book-length study available.[8]

Group-affiliated scholars, regardless of ethnicity, generally offer two arguments to support their claims for the special status of their people. First, they argue that their group can look back on a longer history in

Canada than other immigrant peoples. A second, more substantial argument emphasizes that, after the British and the French, Ukrainians or Germans or Italians constitute the third-largest group in Canada according to census data.

The position taken in this research note is that the creation of the German-Canadians or an assumption of homogeneity of any other group by census-takers or the respective group's historians has only limited factual basis, as the census-data show.[9] Because of the group's diverse origins, I will refer to the "German-language groups." Its case is particularly complicated because the majority of the migrants came to Canada in secondary migrations from East Central, Eastern and Southeastern Europe or from the United States, where their ancestors had settled generations earlier. Even though settlement after the first migration often occurred in compact areas with the explicit intention of maintaining culture, the migrants had been subject to acculturation pressures and processes. They had developed German-Russian, Balkan-German or German-American immigrant cultures, differentiated into numerous variations. In 1973, the German Canadian Yearbook's opening editorial defined "Germans" as "people who were either themselves born and raised where German was spoken as a first language or whose forebears came from such an environment."[10]

The problems of defining "German" ethnicity are well illustrated by the case of an Austrian socialist who migrated to the United States. Arriving in New York in 1910 he was denied a job as editor of the German-language New York *Volkszeitung* whose board rhetorically took an internationalist stand, but whose hiring policy preferred German Germans to Austrian Germans. Later, as editor of the German-language socialist *Cleveland Echo*, he ran into difficulties with the established German-American working-class and middle-class communities because his sentiments, in their opinion, were not "national." Once, when agreeing with Cleveland's Italian socialists, he was called "Spagettifritzi." Who was he then writing for? According to his own words he addressed recently immigrated German proletarians, few of whom came from the Reich, but "from Austria, from Hungary, from the Baltic areas and God knew from which other places. Even German workers from Syria.... To express their feelings and views these workers ... resorted to different usages of the German language.... A simple and clear German consisting of about 850 words and similar to 'basic English' had to be developed to reach all of them."[11] The microcosm of the Cleveland "Germans" consisted of a cultural plurality as did the large group of "Germans" in Canada. What were their backgrounds?

The area in which German was spoken was large and dispersed, and language usage was differentiated by class. Up to 1918, the contiguous core area of German language usage was divided between the Austrian section of the Habsburg empire, the substantial parts of Switzerland, and the "Germanies"; i.e., the literally hundreds of smaller sovereignties recognized by the Treaty of Westphalia in 1648, hammered into slightly over thirty larger ones by Napoleon in 1806, and—after the Habsburg-Hohenzollern competition for leadership—herded into a German Reich under Prussian domination in 1871. Secondly, a Central European German-language culture of the educated classes had emerged, first by migrations eastward since the 12th century, then by journeymen artisans' migrations, and finally by the Berlin and Vienna imperial bureaucracies' usage of German as administrative language. Thirdly, further east, German-language colonies arose as a result of the compact settlement of German agriculturists in the South Russian plains from the 1760s to the 1830s, and Austrian colonization of Balkan territories reconquered from the Ottoman empire. In the towns and cities, only some socio-cultural strata used German: aristocracy, patriciate, and artisans. The disenfranchised native-born majority of peasants, serfs and urban underclasses, with whom the German-language newcomers interacted, spoke the respective local languages, the "vernacular."[12]

This diversity was reflected among "German" immigrants to Canada as was obvious to scholars of the 1930s.[13] The German-language mosaic comprises people divided by dialect, religion, type of migration and nationality. Firstly, the German-Canadian groups consist of three language groups, as Cardinal and Malycky noted: High German, Low German and Pennsylvania German.[14] The regional variants (dialects) or social variants (sociolects) were not necessarily mutually understandable. Secondly, some immigrants had merged ethnicity and religion into a distinct ethno-religious culture. This includes the Mennonite, Hutterite and Amish groups as well as the Moravian Bretheren,[15] few of whom came directly from the German core areas and who combined Dutch, Swiss and German dissenters. They had separated voluntarily from the majority culture in their area of origin and had experienced adaptation to their first host societies reluctantly. Similarly, German-speaking Jews, given the process of group formation in Canada, may have to be categorized with the Jewish group. Thirdly, all other German-speaking migrants from areas outside of the core area of the German language were culturally distinct.[16] Fourthly, those coming in primary migrations from the core area were culturally divided into Swiss, Austrians and Germans, the latter in particular with regional differentiation, as well as from subgroups like Alsatians and Frisians.[17]

The German-speaking peoples, like other groups, came under widely diverging historical circumstances. Their acculturation experience or their retention of ethnic traits has to be conceptualized in terms of a sequence of immigration peaks and troughs, of generations or cohorts, each distinct from the other. Some have undergone a homogenization process in Canada, but this is a Canadian and not a German (or Italian, or Ukrainian) characteristic. The distinction into "generations," commonly used for Ukrainian and Hungarian immigrants, also helps to understand differences in outlook and attitudes among German pre-World War I migrants, those of the interwar years and the post-World War II newcomers. The aggressive role of their country of origin in the two wars caused some to renounce their roots; others who had come before the wars were forced to do so because of enemy alien persecutions and prosecutions in Canada.[18] The formation of ethnic identities in Canada, as in any other receiving society, is thus a product of both the old and the new society.

In terms of generations and regional origin, the "German-Canadian mosaic" consists of the early arrivals ("Lunenburgers" in the 1750s; Pennsylvania Germans since the 1760s; survivors of the German mercenary troops; and loyalists of German background from the mid-Atlantic colonies); of the direct migrants from Germany; of secondary migrants from the United States since the 1780s; of the Danube Swabians, Transylvania Saxons and Russian Germans since the 1870s; of Baltic Germans and Sudeten Germans as a result of the two world wars; and of the "German Germans" of the interwar and post-World War II years.[19] Immigrants from Austria and Switzerland are treated separately by historians from these groups and the countries of origin, as well as in the Canadian Census.[20] Religious groups that once used or still use dialects of the German language but which separated from German mainstream culture have also developed their own historiography. Incorporation of all of the diverse groups within some kind of "German ancestry" or German-language usage thus turns into a struggle over historiographical territory and implies taking positions in group politics. On the other hand, in interaction with Canadian mainstream society as well as with other immigrant groups, some of the diverse German-language newcomers did, indeed, construct one German-Canadian group.

If self-constructed ethnic group status is not necessarily an indicator of group composition, ascribed status on the aggregate level of official Canadian statistics is also misleading.[21] In "ethnic origin" (formerly called "racial origin") statistics, "Germans" account for 5.82 percent of the total Canadian population in 1871 and 6.11 percent in 1971. Swiss and Austrians are listed separately.

The first and main problem is reliance on self-identification within those categories offered by the census questionnaires. It is no surprise that the standing of an ethnic group within the hierarchy of ethnic reputations influences the decision of persons whether to declare themselves to be of a particular ethnic origin. Thus, when public opinion about Germany was low, as during the two World Wars, the numbers of German-Canadians declined substantially from 5.60 percent in 1911 to 3.35 percent in 1921, and from 4.46 percent in 1931 to 4.04 percent in 1941.[22] The percentage remained low in 1951 (4.43 percent). It increased after the massive immigration of the 1950s (218,000) to 5.75 percent in 1961, but when immigration declined in the 1960s (56,000), self-ascription continued to grow, with 6.11 percent of the population declaring German background in 1971. This presumably reflected the improved position and reputation of Germany in the international community and in Canadian public opinion.

The aggregate data for the 19th and 20th century combined provide support for the German-Canadian mosaic's claim to first place after the British and French mosaics. To understand the group's impact on present-day Canada as well as internal group cohesion in the 1980s, the period of arrival has to be taken into account. According to Department of Citizenship and Immigration statistics for 1900-1960, Italians are the largest immigrant group (425,200), followed by the composite German/Austrian group (373,200) and the Ukrainian group (340,739). For the period 1900-1945 Italians were the largest immigrant group, followed by the Jewish and Ukrainian and then by the German/Austrian and Russian groups.[23] From 1946 to 1973, by country of last permanent residence, 708,600 persons came from England, 464,000 from Italy, 315,200 from the Federal Republic of Germany, 207,400 from Scotland and 177,600 from the Netherlands. The post-war German immigrants had to compete for attention with, for example, refugees fleeing Hungary after the 1956 revolt and migrants from the Caribbean.[24]

The second problem, insufficient subdivision of groups, can often be solved by cross-tabulation of census data on ethnicity with those of country of birth or nationality as well as with other sources. More than two thirds of the German-speaking peoples came in secondary migrations from countries with non-German cultures, less than one quarter came directly from Germany, under 10 percent from the German-language areas of Austria and Switzerland (primary migrations).[25] In his study of "the German element (*Deutschtum*)" in the Prairie Provinces, the nationalist German historian Heinz Lehmann estimated that only 12 percent of those counted as "Germans" had come from Germany.[26] In Alberta in 1921, the four largest German-origin groups were Russian-born (34.2 percent), German-born (26.3 percent), U.S.-born (25.6 percent) and Polish-born (13.9 percent).[27] According to Moellmann's study of Montreal in 1926-1931, the German group was split into three sections in the interwar years, the pre-war immigrants (German-Canadians), the post-war newcomers from the German Reich (*Reichsdeutsche*) and the ethnics of German background who came from the areas beyond the contiguous German enthnolinguistic territory in Europe (*Volksdeutsche*). They had to overcome cultural and economic differences to merge into one group. *Volksdeutsche* came without means, while *Reichsdeutsche* came with $50 or more. In consequence the two groups developed different ways of coping with their economic adaptation. They had their separate ethnic organizations and patterns of social relations.[28]

Thirdly, mother tongue and ethnic origin statistics do not match. From 1926 to 1945, 105,000 immigrants declared themselves to be of German, Swiss or Austrian "racial origin," but in the age group of 10 years and older only 61,100 declared German to be their mother tongue. Since children up to 10 years comprised approximately one eighth of all immigrants, this means that at the time of immigration perhaps one third of those aged ten years and over who declared themselves as "German," or were categorized by immigration officials as such, did not speak German.[29] Thus even the terminological change to the more cautious "German-speaking" overemphasizes group size. Those arriving were hyphenated Germans in the process of adding another hyphen to their multiple cultural backgrounds. Not surprisingly, later census data show language retention to be higher among Italians and Ukrainians, lower among the Dutch.

Fourthly, separatist ethno-religious groups have to be deducted from the German "ethnic origin" totals. The 1971 Census listed 126,700 Mennonites and Hutterites of German ethnic background, almost 10 percent of the total for persons of German ethnic origin. The corresponding figure for 1931 was 7.3 percent.[30] Even though these groups strongly stressed their distinctiveness from Russian and other receiving societies, they no longer developed in conjunction with German, Swiss-German, Austrian or Dutch culture. In Canada, they continued to consider themselves distinct from other groups. An Ontario Mennonite farmer, according to his diary, hired Amish, Syrian and German people for help on his farm in the 1910s. All three groups seemed to be equally distinct from his own culture.[31] Although it would have no quantitative impact, it would be worthwhile to investigate the cultural traditions those "Germans" whose religion was Greek Orthodox or Ukrainian Catholic (0.12 percent each of the total group).[32]

A fifth problem in the compilation of ethnic and racial origin statistics is that ethnic origin is reckoned through the male line. This increases the size of all groups which have a surplus of male immigrants who marry women from other groups. According to Moellmann's calculations for the province of Quebec in 1931, the imbalanced sex ratio amounted to 145:100 in the child-bearing age group of 20-39. In that year 169 children were born to German fathers, but only 81 of them had German mothers (47.9 percent), the others having mothers of French (41), British (38), or other origin (9). Before "multiple origins" became a census category in 1981, the immigrant segment of each ethnic group that included out-marrying men was augmented by such a "home-grown" segment.[33]

While it is easy to deconstruct the size and homogeneity of ethnic groups, it is considerably more difficult and perhaps impossible to reconstruct the size of any group from immigration figures. Three time series of immigration figures are available for German-Canadians: the German statistics of emigration to Canada, 1847 to 1937;[34] the immigration statistics of the Department of Citizenship and Immigration (DCI), 1896 to 1961 and later;[35] and the immigration statistics published in the *Canada Year Book* (CYB) and its precursors from the 1860s to the present.[36] The series, which run parallel from 1901 to 1930, yield widely divergent emigration/immigration totals for these three decades: 35,200 (German figures), 61,800 (CYB), or 122,000 (DCI).

The methods of data collection changed over time and were not properly explained. Let us consider the major changes and evaluate the under- or overcount. The German emigration statistics, listing a total of 114,400 immigrants to Canada from 1847 to 1937, undercount emigration to Canada because they exclude emigration via French, Dutch or British ports, from the mid-1800s onward—perhaps 10-15 percent of the total German emigration. They include Jews of German citizenship; Poles from the Prussian partition zone, who were German citizens; and after 1871 Alsatians.[37]

Among Canadian data, cross-tabulation of the series on "citizenship" and "ethnic origin" provides information on cultural changes in earlier migrations, beyond that contained in the self-categorization of ethnic background.[38] From the different data in the *Canada Year Book*, the series "by nationality," later "citizenship," has been used in the above comparisons. The total according to this count stands at 385,560 German immigrants for 1865-1980. This is an overcount because no emigration statistics were compiled, and many arrivals were transit migrants to the United States.[39] The CYB statistics have the advantage that, for the years 1926-1963, when "Austrians" were often included with "Germans" even from a Canadian perspective, they are listed as a separate group in some editions, so that a complete time series for Austrians can be reconstructed. The Department of Citizenship and Immigration, reporting by calendar year, used the vague term "ethnic origin" again. Its figures do not agree with any of the CYB series. They are one third higher than the citizenship statistics of the CYB. Austrians were included with Germans for the years from 1926 to 1933.

This hodgepodge of data makes accurate reconstructions of group sizes impossible. The figures for German, Austrian, and Swiss immigration stand in a relation of 15:3:1 for the period 1901-1960,[40] but Austria was a multiethnic state to 1918 and Switzerland continues to be so. Figures by racial origin do not help: Austrians are categorized (as a separate "race") only into the early 1930s, and throughout the decades some or all Swiss immigrants insisted on calling themselves of "Swiss" origin. The puzzled statisticians noted: "Reported as Swiss origin but evidently one of the constituent races."

From 1926 to 1945, when nationality, racial origin and mother tongue statistics were collected in parallel, 97,900 persons of German racial origin, 61,100 persons 10 years and over of German mother tongue and 24,800 persons of German citizenship were counted. In other words, the "German" group quadruples in size when "race" is used and there are no separate listings for Austrians or Mennonites. One glimpse is provided by the table "Immigrant Populations by Mother Tongue, Birthplace and Sex" of the 1931 Census, which gives as origins of the German-speaking population: German-born 23.5 percent, Austrian-born 7.2 percent, Swiss-born not available, Eastern, East Central and Southeastern Europe 49 percent, other Europe 4.8 percent, United States-born 15.2 percent, South America and rest of the world, 0.2 percent. These data also reveal that of the 39,163 German-born immigrants 6.1 percent (2,363) did not have German as a mother tongue, but English (1,370), Yiddish (332), Polish (180), or other.[41]

The result of both processes, the deconstruction of the exaggerated claims for a special position of Canadians of German origin and the construction of time series by citizenship or mother tongue, is that Germans from Germany were indeed one of the five largest groups of the "allophone" category. The internal multicultural and multi-linguistic composition of these groups—Bavarians, Saxons, Rhinelanders and citizens of the Hanseatic towns in the North, to name only a few—reveals the existence of a rich internal mosaic despite the pressures for a melting-pot, through ascription of "Germanness" by other groups in society or by interested group members.

A sophisticated sociological study of ethnic identity retention in Toronto, 1977-79, supports the contention that persons of German ethnic origin lose their distinctiveness comparatively quickly. Concerning the external aspects of ethnic identity, they rank consistently in the lowest third in a comparison of nine groups. They rank even lower where internal identity is concerned. Of Isajiw's four dimensions of identity, the cognitive one in particular may help to explain why identity retention is low among German-origin Canadians. It "includes, first, self-images and images of one's group. These may be stereotypes.... It also includes knowledge of one's group's heritage and its historical past ...[and] finally ... knowledge of one's group's values."[42] For the heterogeneous "German" groups, the shared past was generations back. Each of the many groups came with its own variant of culture. If, out of this heterogeneity, a German group was to emerge in Canada, a process of homogenization, of cultural change from a lived specific Russo-, Polish-, Austro-, or German-German culture to a Canadian-German average was required. If acculturation is necessary to fit into an ethnic group, recent newcomers may choose to acculturate directly into the multicultural mainstream of the receiving culture.

## MULTICULTURALISM IN THE PRESENT

In the past, the process of acculturation was directed toward one of the two majority cultures, which in turn responded to the newcomers, whether turn-of-the-century Italians needed as workers in Montreal or Ukrainians needed as settlers on the prairies. Similarly, German-, Swiss-, and Austrian-origin immigrant cultures have merged into Canadian culture in this process common to all Canadian groups. Even the first arrivals, French and English, changed their lifestyles to fit the new surroundings. In the present, the relationships between cultures have reached a new level of acceptance and interaction. Most Canadians do prefer to live in "the Canadian mosaic" rather than under Anglo- or Franco-conformity or in ethnic separatism. While some decry the loss of ethnic identity, as do some German-origin Canadians, others complain about being assigned to ethnic slots.[43] Pieces of a mosaic are glued or cemented into a defined space. Culture, whether ethnic, Anglo, French or Canadian, is always in motion. It is as full of colour as a mosaic but as changing as a kaleidoscope, a kaleidoscope to which new elements are being added constantly. In the past, the multicultural contributions appear to be fixed as in a mosaic, but in the present it is obvious that the multiple parts interact, change, and move constantly. Canadian society now is a culturally interactive whole of multiple groups engaged in actively structured courses of development. This new type of interaction deserves more differentiated attention than it has received in talkshows and thirty-second soundbites. In this concluding section we will therefore analyze the multicultural "Canadianness" of the 1990s.

The cultures which immigrants bring with them in their hearts, minds, and actions are as changeable as the multifaceted Canadian one which they enter. They leave societies of origin because they are pushed out, because they see few or no options for their lives. Thus critics of ethnic politicking are right to point out that the old societies were no models to be reestablished. Emigration or flight, however, is often not from a way of life but from particularly oppressive or constricting societies. After migration the everyday way of life develops as an exchange between a remembered past, the lived present, and the ever important hopes for the future.

Processes of cultural change are Canadian history. The French and British in Lower and Upper Canada had to adapt to an environment different from that of their home villages and towns, and adapt they did.

The Ukrainians who founded self-help organizations at the turn of the century were reacting to their new environment. In the process of organizing as Ukrainians, they established a basis in the new society that permitted them to stay under adverse conditions and even to prosper. Over time they became Ukrainian-Canadians. Without such networks of support, migrants in times of crisis would have to go back to the help of their old-world family. Political scientists view diversity, view such interest or lobbying groups as necessary elements of the democratic political process. Immigrants' self-organization could involve the emergence of a fully structured ethnic community, "clannishness" in the eyes of assimilationists, "institutional completeness," as sociologists call it.[44] From this solid base they could negotiate with the receiving society and achieve what as individual ethnics they could not have hoped for. They finally became Canadians of Ukrainian—or German, or other—descent, an identity that combines a distant shared past with an active new future.

Both, those who want to retain their Canadian culture in its present form, and those who cling to their past culture of origin, do so for equally valid reasons. Willingly or not, by living together they enter negotiating processes and develop new identities. Cultural retention is a slowdown of changes to permit both a withering of older identities without psychological damage and the development of new identities without demands for unconditional surrender. New cultures need as much respect as those who are already established expect for their ways from the newcomers.

The active participation of many cultures in the making of Canada was justly acknowledged when the Royal Commission on Bilingualism and Biculturalism, as a result of the lobbying of the older European ethnic groups, decided to add the famous fourth volume to its Report of 1968. In its first stage, the goals of the 1971 policy of "multiculturalism in a bilingual framework" were linguistic pluralism for the two "official" groups, and help in entering Canadian society for the others. Multiculturalism was to be a process of interaction, with support for people's development, but not for static concepts of home culture. This important implication, one Canadian identity made up of all its constituent groups, seems to have been forgotten in later debates.[45] Unknowingly, some present critics of the policy are merely asking for a return to the concept that was originally embedded in it.

The second stage of multiculturalism began with the transfer of the concept into a federal policy after 1971. Many tasks lay ahead to transform existing structures to conform with the popular view that there was more to Canada than Anglo or French culture to which ethnic group cultures were added. For example, in the realm of education, new schoolbooks and college texts had to be written to do justice to multiple inputs into Canadian society. The children of newcomers were to receive both, help with English or French as a second language and respect for their mother tongue. While doors were opened to newcomers, they had to cross the threshold on their own, just as members of the older groups like the German-language people, had done. Over time, when some Euro-Canadians seemed to react with fear and hostility to skin colours other than white, the policy also sought to strengthen anti-racism and to ensure equal opportunities for all. Viewed in a worldwide context, Canadian policies toward newcomers rank high in terms of humanitarian approaches and practical efficiency. If immigrant groups in Germany, Switzerland, and Austria would receive as much respect for their distinctive contributions as immigrants from these societies did in Canada, present tensions there could certainly be eased.

When the policy of multiculturalism was first announced, its retentive nature—best described as a desire to celebrate diversity—was emphasized over other aspects like development, evolution, and interaction. This is also the approach of ethnic group publications celebrating their specific characteristics. Although diversity increased society's options, the concept of a unified pluralist Canada was relegated to the background. Funding for cultural expression broader than merely Anglo and Québécois brought forth a wide range of important teaching materials. But over time administrative allocation of funds began to be guided by group interests rather than by considerations of excellence.[46] Support reached cultural gatekeepers and ethnic organizations instead of providing for an interactive Canadian culture. Established groups need no support once imbalances in educational materials and academic research have been rectified, whereas newly arriving immigrant groups need help for a limited period of time, once the "Canadian" materials have become integrated. Children in school want to confront their own time; they are being educated for their future; they are not receptacles for memories of former times that perhaps were important to their grandparents. One generation's cultural retention, often of petrified or quaint parts of the heritage, shifts the burden of adjustment to the next generation.

Many aspects of "Heritage Culture"—folk dances, for example—are no longer part of modern societies. They are remnants of a past that the forefathers and mothers of today's Canadians of Ukrainian or German descent left generations ago. Bavarian Lederhosen bands are not really typical of German culture today. What is being preserved is a Canadian construction of visible aspects of cultures of the past—symbolic ethnicity. More recent immigrant groups, on the other hand, still use cultural practices of their societies of origin in everyday life and are still in the process of adaptation. The present debate about multiculturalism perhaps reflects the uneasiness of members of some groups, including a few German-Canadians who feel that, over the course of time, their particular cultural contribution has receded into the background.

In retrospect, it is evident that in the 1960s—before multiculturalism—several dramatic developments coincided in producing social change. In Quebec, the Quiet Revolution reformed the entire society. Economic factors, the position of the Church and the educational system were brought in line with the rest of Canada. With regard to culture, on the other hand, the heritage, the concept of survivance, was stressed. Also in the 1960s, in all of Canada, a new self-assertiveness began to express itself. Schools lost their Anglo-exclusionism and provincialism. Universities moved from a position that was marginal in international scholarship to a strong position of their own. Because of their impact on the future generation and policymaking, the changes in education and research were of particular importance. With a growing awareness of these profound changes, some Canadians became uneasy and, as a scapegoating tactic, began to fault multiculturalism policies for assumed problems in society or the decline of their own group. Cultural pluralism for smaller resident groups like Basques, Scots, and Bretons is also discussed in European countries. A new awareness of cultural integrity has spread. While in Europe the debate is about a nation's ability to accommodate diversity, the debate in Canada, it seems, is about a new multifaceted Canadianness, replacing either conformity or biculturalism.

Some of the criticism of multiculturalism probably hinges on the relationship of Euro-Canadians to the cultural heritage and the rights of what are visible minorities or "non-white" groups—Native Canadians, Afro-Canadians and Asian-Canadians—all three groups internally as heterogeneous as Euro-Canadians. "Race," a concept with no scientific basis, was constructed to justify the domination of "whites" over "non-whites" using colour of skin as a criterion. But multiple origins included marriages between people of different skin colour. Would a child of Euro-Asian heritage give alternating answers when filling out forms in which "race" has to be indicated? In the darkest period of German history people were designated according to ancestry as "quarter-Jews" or "half-Jews." In the United States census, the "one drop"-rule still applies: one black ancestor generations back makes a person "non-white," an absurdity that merely reflects racism and power relationships. Recent Congressional hearings indicate that this may be changed before the next census; recent opinion polls in Canada indicate that "visible minorities" consider themselves "Canadian" and nothing else.[47]

In Canada, the difficulties of accepting the change, of accepting one Canadian cultural identity are illustrated by the census. Only in 1951— eighty-five years after Dominion status—was an ethnic-origin category "Canadian" inserted into the questionnaires, and census-takers were instructed to mark it only "when a person insists." In an age of increasing national chauvinism this may be considered a friendly sign of national modesty. But it prevented a count of those who had moved from their original identities to a new Canadian consciousness. Secondly, only in 1981 was a category "multiple origin" introduced into the census-forms. It was marked by 11 percent of the respondents in 1981, by 26 percent in 1986, by 29 percent in 1991.

Statistics Canada has realized that its yardstick, "ethnic origin," has become useless for measuring the size of Canada's component parts. With respect to the 1991 Census, attempts to change the census forms were rejected by politicians and by specific cultural interest groups who want to keep their numbers separate and large so that they may continue to receive cultural funding. This is invented ethnicity as a money-making scheme. A 1988 trial run by Statistics Canada of a form with a mark-in box for Canadian ethnic origin and one for Canadian ethnic identity showed that the former was marked by 36 percent of the respondents, the latter by 53 percent.[48] Canada is less diverse than it appears to some. Most inhabitants of Canada today consider themselves Canadian citizens with a Canadian identity and with multiple cultural backgrounds.

In conclusion, the present Canadianness is a result of far-reaching changes in Canadian society in the 1960s and after. Multicultural policies and practices have been one aspect of these changes. For newcomers they have facilitated entry into the society; for established residents they have created options beyond conformity to English or French models. Jointly, the changes and the multicultural options have brought about a new identity. The debate about a contribution of German-language groups would have been well placed when the Bi- and Bi-Commission asked for research. Now, contribution history is a thing of the past; what is needed are interdisciplinary studies of acculturation. The cry, "Don't call me ethnic," is as justified as attempts of German-language Canadians to remember their past without creating an artificial group construct. Identity is self-determined, whether Canadian, ethnic, or recent newcomer.[49]

## ENDNOTES

1.   The research since the 1960s has been reviewed in John W. Berry and J.A. Laponce, *Ethnicity and Culture in Canada: The Research Landscape* (Toronto, 1994). See also Dirk Hoerder, "Ethnic Studies in Canada from the 1880s to 1962: A Historiographical Perspective and Critique," *Canadian Ethnic Studies* (hereafter *CES*) 26 (1994), 1-18.

2.   In 1931 and 1941 Ukrainians had more speakers than ethnics (112 and 102 percent respectively) because of their integration of Polish, Slovak and Belorussian speakers. Paul Mingus, ed., *Sounds Canadian: Languages and Cultures in Multiethnic Society* (Toronto, 1975), 32.

3.   See the research by Harney, Iacovetta, Perin, Sturino, Scardellato, Zucchi and others. An excellent introduction to this material is Roberto Perin and Franc Sturino, eds., *Arrrangiarsi: The Italian Immigration Experience in Canada* (Montreal, 1989).

4.   Hugh MacLennan, *Two Solitudes* (Toronto, 1945); Michael Greenstein, *Third Solitudes: Tradition and Discontinuity in Jewish-Canadian Literature* (Kingston, 1989); Irving M. Abella and Harold Troper, *None Is Too Many: Canada and the Jews of Europe, 1933-1948* (Toronto, 1982).

5.   Gerhard P. Bassler, "Silent or Silenced Co-Founders of Canada? Reflections on the History of German Canadians," *Canadian Ethnic Studies* 22 (1990), 38-46, quote p. 38; Rudolf A. Helling et al., *A Socio-Economic History of German-Canadians. They, too, Founded Canada* (Wiesbaden, 1984), does not claim "special status" for the group but "describes its participation ... in the building of this country," p. 15. Robert H. Keyserlingk, "The Canadian Government's Attitude Towards Germans and German Canadians in World War Two," *Canadian Ethnic Studies* 16 (1984), 16-28.

6.   Donald Avery and Bruno Ramirez, "European Immigrant Workers in Canada: Ethnicity, Militancy and State Repression," in Dirk Hoerder et al., eds., *Roots of the Transplanted*, 2 vols. (Boulder and New York, 1994), 419.

7.   Hartmut Froeschle and Lothar Zimmermann, *German Canadiana: A Bibliography*, vol. 11 of the *German-Canadian Yearbook* (Toronto, 1990).

8.   Heinz Lehmann, *The German Canadians 1750-1937. Immigration, Settlement and Culture*, translated, edited and introduced by Gerhard P. Bassler from Lehmann's

*Zur Geschichte des Deutschtums in Kanada* (1931) and *Das Deutschtum in Westkanada* (1939)(St. John's, 1986). See also Bassler's *The German Canadian Mosaic Today and Yesterday: Identities, Roots, and Heritage* (Ottawa, 1991).

9.  One little-known publication of 1983 demanded differentiation among areas of origin, taking Lunenburg, N.S., as an example: Peter G. Liddell, ed., *German Canadian Studies: Critical Approaches* (Vancouver, 1983); see esp. the essays by Manfred Richter, "Who Are the German Canadians? Looking at the Canadian Census and the Social Sciences for Answers," pp. 42-48; David Artiss, "Who Are the German-Canadians: One Ethnic Group or Several?" pp. 49-55, and Herminio Schmidt, "The German-Canadians and Their Umbilical Cord," pp. 71-77. According-ing to Schmidt, p. 74, segments of the German group "have religiously expended an enormous amount of energy for what they say is 'the preservation of the German culture.' In reality those were the people who had most problems in freeing themselves from the umbilical cord of the mother country."

10. Froeschle and Zimmermann, *Bibliography*, 7.

11. Josef N. Jodlbauer's autobiography, *13 Jahre in Amerika [1910-1923]* translated by Dirk Hoerder (Vienna,1995), pp. 74-75.

12. For an excellent view of this heterodox pattern at a glace, see Paul Robert Magocsi, *Historical Atlas of East Central Europe* (Toronto, 1993), pp. 104-06.

13. Research on the M.A. or Ph.D. level does indicate a readiness to differentiate: studies on the Bessarabian German dialect, on language differentiation among Low German groups, or on Galician German language usage show that source materials from which to proceed are available.

14. Clive H. Cardinal and Alexander Malycky, ed., "German-Canadian Creative Literature: A Preliminary Check List," CES, 1 (1969), 31.

15. Andrew Gregorovich in his seminal *Canadian Ethnic Groups Bibliography* (Toronto, 1972), xvi, differentiated between Swiss, Austrians and Germans and among the latter between "German, Amish, Hutterite, Mennonite, [and] Pennsylvania German" people.

16. For example, Baltic Germans, Russian Germans, Transylvania Saxons, Danubian Swabians, or non-Mennonite Pennsylvania Dutch.

17. *The Harvard Encyclopedia of American Ethnic Groups* (Cambridge, MA, 1980) differentiates between Germans, Austrians, Swiss, as well as Alsatians, Frisians, Amish, Hutterites, Germans from Russia and Pennsylvania Germans.

18. Voluntarily or involuntarily many of those who declared themselves "German" in the 1911 Census changed to "Dutch" in 1921.

19. For a survey see Hartmut Froeschle, *Die Deutschen in Kanada: Eine Volksgruppe im Wandel* (Vienna, 1987).

20. Hans Chmelar, *Höhepunkte der österreichischen Auswanderung* (Vienna, 1974),

esp. pp. 31-34 and 61-64; Emile Henri Bovay, *Le Canada et les Suisses 1604-1974* (Fribourg, 1976).

21. The general problems of the "ethnic origin" statistics have been discussed repeatedly: N.B. Ryder, "The Interpretation of Origin Statistics," *Canadian Journal of Economics and Political Science*, 21 (1955), 466-79; Warren E. Kalbach and Wayne W. McVey, *The Demographic Bases of Canadian Society* (Toronto: McGraw Hill, 1971), chap. 6; Warren E. Kalbach, *The Impact of Immigration on Canada's Population*, 1961 Census Monograph (Ottawa, 1970).

22. One author added Germans, Austrians and Netherlanders into a "German element" category and thus started with a 6.67 percent share in 1871 and even in 1921 still arrived at a 5.92 percent share of the total population. Albert Moellmann, *Das Deutschtum in Montreal*, Schriften des Instituts für Grenz- und Auslandsdeutschtum an der Universitaet Marburg, no. 11 (Jena, 1937), p. 88. This book was based on his M.A. thesis, "The Germans in Canada: Occupational and Social Adjustment of German Immigrants in Canada" (McGill University, 1934).

23. For the most recent data (1986) see *Ethnic Diversity in Canada* (Ottawa, 1990), Tables 2, 4, 10 and Appendix. By place of birth, 189,560 persons from Germany were counted among the immigrant population (4.9 percent as compared to 9.4 percent for Italy), whereas there were 348,520 speakers of German as mother tongue (with a low percentage in the age group of 19 years and younger).

24. Department of Manpower and Immigration, *Canadian Immigration and Population Study* [Green Paper on Immigration], vol. 3, Table 3.2 (Ottawa, 1974).

25. Lehmann, *The German-Canadians*, p. 133; Moellmann, *Deutschtum*, p. 115; *Census of Canada* 1931, vol. 1, pp. 1258-59, Table 81 "Immigrant Population by Mother Tongue, Birthplace and Sex, 1931."

26. In the context of German politics after the rise of the NSDAP to power, Lehmann and Moellmann were moderate in their emphasis on "Germanness." Moellmann, while employing the contemporary politically loaded terminology of *Reichsdeutsche* (Germans of the Reich) and *Volksdeutsche* (Germans living outside of the Reich), worked in the tradition of the McGill University studies in economics and sociology. Both, however, tended to consider groups "German" which might contain some ethnic Germans. Other authors annexed Austro-Hungarian, Russian and Dutch immigrants, "most of whom speak and read German," as claimed by Gotthard L. Maron, editor of *Der Nordwesten*, the largest German-Canadian newspaper, in the booklet, *Facts About the Germans in Canada* (Winnipeg, 1913), p. 30. He thereby increased the 1911 Census figure of 403,000 by about 25 percent "to more than 500,000."

27. Elizabeth Barbara Gerwin, "A Survey of the German-speaking Population in Alberta," (unpublished M.A. thesis, University of Alberta, Edmonton, 1938),

as quoted in Jean Burnet, *Next-Year Country* (Toronto, 1951), p. 172. The smaller groups are not included.

28. Moellmann, *Montreal*, pp. iii, 32-35, 46, passim.

29. *Canada Year Book* (hereafter *CYB*) 1926-1947, Tables "Mother Tongues of Immigrants" and "Racial Origins of Immigrants." Figures for the age group 0-9 are available in *CYB* 1927-28 and 1930 for all immigrants. Their share amounts to 12.6 percent.

30. *Census of Canada* 1971, vol. 1.3: Table 1 and vol. 1.4: Table 18 and graph "Percentage Distribution of Specified Religious Denominations by Selected Ethnic Groups, Canada, 1971." Census of Canada, 1931, vol. 1, Table 3, "Racial Origin ..."

31. James M. Nyce ed., *The Gordon C. Eby Diaries, 1911-13: Chronicle of a Mennonite Farmer*, (Toronto, 1982), pp. 24ff (Syrian), 162ff (Amish), 98ff (German).

32. *Census* 1971, vol. 1.4, Table 18.

33. Moellmann, *Montreal*, pp. 115-116. Cf. *Census* 1931, Table 3.

34. The German figures refer to emigration via the ports of Hamburg and Bremen, 1847-70 (according to statistics of the two state governments). From 1871 to 1937 the figures are from *Statistisches Jahrbuch des Deutschen Reiches* and refer to total emigration per fiscal year. The 1871-1918 figures refer to Germany in its borders of 1871, figures thereafter to Germany in its 1918 borders. For a summary of the information to 1900 and references to earlier studies see Peter Marschalck, *Deutsche Ueberseewanderung im 19. Jahrhundert* (Stuttgart, 1973), pp. 48-50.

35. Department of Citizenship and Immigration, *Immigration Statistics 1896 to 1961* (Ottawa, n.d.) and subsequent reports. This publication lacks information on how the statistics were compiled.

36. *Canada Year Book*, published privately 1867-1879, published by the Department of Agriculture as Statistical Year-Book, 1885 (vol. 1) to 1904, and with continuous numbering by the Census and Statistics Office since 1905. From the 1860s to the 1890s data on ethnic groups are incomplete. Collection of data varied from fiscal years to calendar years. The collection of data for the several series is not sufficiently explained. Repeatedly, later editions give figures for earlier years without explanation for the changes.

37. Figures from Wilhelm Moenckmeier, *Die deutsche ueberseeische Auswanderung* (Jena, 1912), pp. 192-93, 206-08; Friedrich Burgdoerfer, "Die Wanderungen ueber die deutschen Reichsgrenzen im letzten Jahrhundert," *Allgemeines Statistisches Archiv*, 20 (1930), 161-96, 383-419, 537-51.

38. In 1926 the collection of data was expanded to include immigrant arrivals by mother tongue (to 1946), by racial (later: ethnic) origin (to 1966) and by country of birth (to 1970). Since 1946 figures have been available by country of last permanent residence.

39. The exasperated statisticians themselves once omitted immigration figures as entirely "untrustworthy." *CYB*, 1892, p. 112.

40. For Switzerland see Bovay, *Le Canada et les Suisses*, p. 105, based on Canadian figures; for Austria see Chmelar, *Höhepunkte*, 61-64.

41. *Census* 1931, vol. 1, pp. 1258-59, Table 81.

42. Wsevolod W. Isajiw, *Ethnic Identity Retention* (Research Paper No. 125, Centre for Urban and Community Studies, University of Toronto, 1981), p. 46.

43. Neil Bissoondath, *Selling Illusions. The Cult of Multiculturalism in Canada* (Markham ON, 1994).

44. Raymond Breton, "Institutional Completeness of Ethnic Communities and the Personal Relations of Immigrants," *American Journal of Sociology* 70 (1964), 193-205.

45. Announcement of Implementation of the Policy of Multiculturalism within a Bilingual Framework. *Canada. Parliament. House of Commons. Debates*, 8 Oct. 1971, pp. 8545-48, 8580-85.

46. One reviewer of a publication on German-Canadians called it a "harvest of stones" that certainly did not merit funding under the multiculturalism program. *Zeitschrift der Gesellschaft für Kanada-Studien* 10 (1990), 134-35.

47. J. Paul Grayson et al., *The Social Construction of "Visible Minority" for Students of Chinese Origin* (Institute for Social Research, York University, 1994); Lawrence Wright, "One Drop of Blood," *New Yorker* 70, no. 22 (25 July 1994), 49-55.

48. Monica Boyd, *Measuring Ethnicity: The Roles of People, Policies and Politics and Social Science Research* (Lectures and Papers in Ethnicity No. 11, University of Toronto, Feb. 1994).

49. This interpretation is also supported by a study of sociologists at the University of Calgary, who find similar political behavior between older generations, whether of immigrant or native background, and younger generations, whether Canadian or foreign-born.

II

DEMOGRAPHIC PATTERNS OF
AUSTRIAN CANADIANS, 1900-1991

*Gertrud Neuwirth and John de Vries*
*Carleton University*

TO ARRIVE AT SOME REASONABLE estimates of the number of Austrians who have settled in Canada during this century, two sources of statistics are available: immigration statistics which give the "flow," as it were, of immigrants entering Canada, and the population census which portrays population characteristics including the ethno-cultural structure of Canadian society. Census data are commonly referred to as "stock data."

However, for several reasons, the two data sources are not, strictly speaking, comparable. Firstly, immigration statistics only give the yearly number of immigrants, but no data are collected on emigration. Thus, it is impossible to say show how many immigrants have returned to their home country or moved to the United States. The population census has been conducted once every ten years, in years ending in "1"; beginning in 1956, a quinquennial census has also been added.[1] Census data are based on the number of permanent residents of Canada at the time the census was taken (a *de jure* census). Secondly, both data sources reflect political considerations and contemporary government priorities, as well as the geopolitical realities of the day and the state of (social) scientific thinking. Thus, early population data may refer to political entities, such as the Austrian-Hungarian Empire, which no longer exist. Moreover, immigration statistics and census data do not use the same definitions or categories. To complicate matters further, the definitions used in each of the data sources have changed repeatedly during this century. Thus, immigration statistics and census data allow for different definitions as to who is to be counted as an Austrian. Thirdly, even if *prima facie* certain categories appear to be the same, the manner in which the information was collected differs. Immigration statistics are based on the information given, together with supporting documents, by the immigrant in his/her application to the Canadian immigration officer. For most of this century, census forms were completed by enumerators on the basis of information provided by the head of household; beginning with the 1971 census, the forms are now filled out by a member of the household, usually but not necessarily the head of the household her/himself.

## IMMIGRATION TO CANADA FROM 1900 TO 1945

Since its colonial beginnings, Canada has relied on the contribution of immigrants to its economic development and population growth. However, depending on the historical context, different economic and/or political criteria have been applied in admitting and selecting immigrants. Following Confederation, the Canadian government proclaimed the first Immigration Act in 1870 and continued to pursue an immigration policy which, prior to Confederation, was initiated by the British Colonial Office[2] and which encouraged the immigration of European settlers.[3] Indeed, the government's economic priorities are clearly reflected in the decision to put the Immigration Branch, established by the 1870 Act, under the Department of Agriculture. The transfer in 1892 of the Immigration Branch to the Department of Mines and Resources is indicative of the same emphasis, since immigrants were now considered as one among several potential resources.

However, despite these economic priorities, political considerations —namely the attempt to build Canada as a white settler society— defined who were to be considered "desirable" immigrants. Promotion of immigration was only allowed in the British Isles, where immigrants were offered assisted passage and cheap land as inducements. As the imposition in 1885 of a head tax on Chinese immigrants shows, persons considered to be racially and culturally unassimilable were discouraged from coming.[4] At the beginning of the twentieth century, a massive settlement program was introduced under Clifford Sifton, in order to open up the Western provinces.[5] Immigration began to take off in 1903 with some 130,000 persons entering, peaked with about 400,000 arriving in 1913 and, as is to be expected, dropped sharply during the World War I period. Thus, between 1900 and 1914 immigration reached nearly 3 million persons.[6] Immigration from Austria has a somewhat similar pattern.

*Table 1. Annual number of immigrants from Austria, classified by ethnic origin, country of last permanent residence, citizenship, country of birth and total Canadian immigration, 1901-1991*

| year | Austrians | | | | total |
|------|---------------|-----------|-------------|-------|-------|
|      | ethnic origin | residence | citizenship | birth |       |
| 1901 | n/a | n/a | 320 | n/a | 55747 |
| 1902 | n/a | n/a | 781 | n/a | 89102 |
| 1903 | n/a | n/a | 516 | n/a | 138660 |
| 1904 | n/a | n/a | 837 | n/a | 131252 |
| 1905 | n/a | n/a | 1324 | n/a | 141465 |
| 1906 | n/a | n/a | 562 | n/a | 211653 |
| 1907 | n/a | n/a | 1899 | n/a | 272409 |
| 1908 | n/a | n/a | 1830 | n/a | 143326 |
| 1909 | n/a | n/a | 4195 | n/a | 173694 |
| 1910 | n/a | n/a | 7891 | n/a | 286839 |
| 1901-1910 | n/a | n/a | 20155 | n/a | 1658828 |
| 1911 | n/a | n/a | 4871 | n/a | 331288 |
| 1912 | n/a | n/a | 1050 | n/a | 375756 |
| 1913 | n/a | n/a | 3147 | n/a | 400870 |
| 1914 | n/a | n/a | 502 | n/a | 150484 |
| 1915 | n/a | n/a | 15 | n/a | 36665 |
| 1916 | n/a | n/a | 1 | n/a | 55914 |
| 1917 | n/a | n/a | 0 | n/a | 72910 |
| 1918 | n/a | n/a | 0 | n/a | 41845 |
| 1919 | n/a | n/a | 5 | n/a | 107698 |
| 1920 | n/a | n/a | 26 | n/a | 138824 |
| 1911-1920 | n/a | n/a | 9617 | n/a | 1712254 |
| 1921 | n/a | n/a | 14 | n/a | 91728 |
| 1922 | n/a | n/a | 23 | n/a | 64224 |
| 1923 | n/a | n/a | 82 | n/a | 133729 |
| 1924 | n/a | n/a | 75 | n/a | 124164 |
| 1925 | n/a | 154 | 177 | 257 | 84907 |
| 1926 | n/a | 530 | 849 | 905 | 135982 |
| 1927 | n/a | 759 | 1389 | 1481 | 158886 |
| 1928 | n/a | 509 | 1161 | 1222 | 166783 |
| 1929 | n/a | 512 | 1053 | 1089 | 164993 |
| 1930 | n/a | n/a | 663 | 727 | 104806 |
| 1921-1930 | n/a | 2464 | 5486 | 5681 | 1230202 |

36

| Year | | | | | |
|---|---|---|---|---|---|
| 1931 | n/a | n/a | 67 | 99 | 27530 |
| 1932 | n/a | n/a | 45 | 75 | 20591 |
| 1933 | n/a | n/a | 46 | 53 | 14382 |
| 1934 | n/a | n/a | 30 | 54 | 12476 |
| 1935 | n/a | n/a | 29 | 47 | 11277 |
| 1936 | n/a | n/a | 40 | 47 | 11643 |
| 1937 | n/a | n/a | 40 | 50 | 15101 |
| 1938 | n/a | n/a | 37 | 78 | 17244 |
| 1939 | n/a | n/a | 2 | 102 | 16994 |
| 1940 | n/a | n/a | 0 | 41 | 11324 |
| 1931-1940 | n/a | n/a | 336 | 646 | 158562 |
| 1941 | n/a | n/a | 0 | n/a | 9329 |
| 1942 | n/a | n/a | 0 | 7 | 7576 |
| 1943 | n/a | n/a | 0 | 11 | 8504 |
| 1944 | n/a | n/a | 0 | 22 | 12801 |
| 1945 | n/a | n/a | 0 | 75 | 22722 |
| 1946 | n/a | n/a | 25 | 302 | 71719 |
| 1947 | n/a | n/a | 72 | 150 | 64127 |
| 1948 | n/a | n/a | 151 | 919 | 125414 |
| 1949 | n/a | n/a | 349 | 1329 | 95217 |
| 1950 | n/a | n/a | 395 | 754 | 73912 |
| 1941-1950 | n/a | n/a | 992 | 3569 | 491321 |
| 1951 | n/a | n/a | 3628 | 4091 | 194391 |
| 1952 | n/a | n/a | 2867 | 3112 | 164498 |
| 1953 | 3612 | n/a | 4224 | 4168 | 168868 |
| 1954 | 3877 | n/a | 4597 | 4346 | 154227 |
| 1955 | 1835 | 2871 | 1997 | 1996 | 109946 |
| 1956 | 2948 | 4330 | 3193 | 3126 | 164857 |
| 1957 | 2293 | 5714 | 2498 | 2620 | 282164 |
| 1958 | 905 | 4544 | 1033 | 1158 | 124851 |
| 1959 | 748 | 1510 | 897 | 975 | 106928 |
| 1960 | 953 | 2038 | 1102 | 1077 | 104111 |
| 1951-1960 | 17171 | 21007 | 26036 | 26669 | 1574841 |
| 1961 | 641 | 1131 | 650 | 648 | 71689 |
| 1962 | 506 | 778 | 457 | 485 | 74586 |
| 1963 | 588 | 799 | 529 | 565 | 93151 |
| 1964 | 751 | 1099 | 658 | 680 | 112606 |
| 1965 | 819 | 1472 | 770 | 803 | 146758 |
| 1966 | 941 | 2313 | 856 | 907 | 194743 |
| 1967 | n/a | 2745 | 1044 | 1099 | 222876 |
| 1968 | n/a | 8125 | 787 | 862 | 183974 |

| | | | | |
|---|---|---|---|---|
| 1969 | n/a | 2083 | 504 | 598 | 161531 |
| 1970 | n/a | 745 | 431 | 494 | 147713 |
| 1961-1970 | 4246 | 21290 | 6686 | 7141 | 1409627 |
| | | | | |
| 1971 | n/a | 407 | 306 | 360 | 121900 |
| 1972 | n/a | 365 | 251 | 285 | 122006 |
| 1973 | n/a | 764 | 286 | 328 | 184200 |
| 1974 | n/a | 780 | 366 | 410 | 218465 |
| 1975 | n/a | 724 | 291 | 332 | 187881 |
| 1976 | n/a | 753 | 277 | 317 | 149429 |
| 1977 | n/a | 564 | 180 | 209 | 114914 |
| 1978 | n/a | 495 | 194 | 198 | 86313 |
| 1979 | n/a | 176 | 184 | 184 | 112096 |
| 1980 | n/a | 240 | 234 | 232 | 143117 |
| 1971-1980 | n/a | 5268 | 2569 | 2855 | 1440321 |
| | | | | |
| 1981 | n/a | 246 | 238 | 270 | 128618 |
| 1982 | n/a | 366 | 201 | 360 | 121147 |
| 1983 | n/a | 143 | 117 | 180 | 89157 |
| 1984 | n/a | 128 | 127 | 149 | 88239 |
| 1985 | n/a | 170 | 165 | 189 | 84302 |
| 1986 | n/a | 201 | 196 | 206 | 99219 |
| 1987 | n/a | 294 | 265 | 285 | 152098 |
| 1988 | n/a | 218 | 197 | 225 | 161929 |
| 1989 | n/a | 259 | 227 | 238 | 192001 |
| 1990 | n/a | 195 | 158 | 194 | 214230 |
| 1981-1990 | n/a | 2220 | 1891 | 2296 | 1330940 |
| 1991 | n/a | 202 | 189 | 183 | 230781 |

As Table 1 shows, their numbers began to increase as well but peaked somewhat earlier. Between 1900 and 1919, altogether 29,451 Austrian citizens immigrated to Canada, 12,492 during the first decade and 16,959 between 1910 and 1913.

However, these figures have to be interpreted with great caution. Immigration statistics for these early years only give the immigrants' country of citizenship. Most of the immigrants during this period came from Southern or Eastern Europe rather than from the British Isles. It is likely, therefore, that at least some of the Austrian citizens came from different parts of the Austrian-Hungarian Empire and not from Austria proper. Indeed, the influx of large numbers of immigrants from Southern and Eastern Europe persuaded the government to encourage immigration from the United Kingdom.[7]

In the years following World War I, that is between 1919 and 1929, immigration to Canada began to increase again substantially amounting, with some fluctuations, to a yearly intake of over 100,000 persons. However, possibly for both economic and political reasons, such as opposition to immigration in the West, several orders-in-council, issued during this period, restricted the classes of admissible immigrants primarily to bona-fide agriculturalists.[8] In the absence of documentary evidence, the impact which these restrictions might have had on potential immigrants from Austria cannot be ascertained. Nevertheless, it is worth noting that between 1919 and 1924 only 229 Austrian citizens arrived in Canada. It was only in 1925 that immigration from Austria increased again.

However, as Table 1 shows, the issue as to who should count as "Austrian" becomes rather complex with the introduction of two new categories, namely: the immigrant's "country of last residence" and the immigrant's "country of birth," in addition to "citizenship." The figures in each of the three categories show a similar trend of a more or less pronounced increase of immigration in each of the years from 1926 to 1929. The number of immigrants is largest for immigrants born in Austria, with 4,953 persons entering Canada during these four years; the number is slightly lower for Austrian citizens (with 4,629), but, with 2,464, is least pronounced for immigrants whose last country of residence was Austria.

The classification of the immigrants' country of last residence is relatively unproblematic. However, since, except for children, all the immigrants must have been born under the Austrian-Hungarian monarchy, the question arises as to how, on the basis of available documents, immigration officials interpreted and classified the immigrants' country of birth and citizenship. In view of the large discrepancies in numbers, it is likely that "country of birth" does not only include immigrants who were born inside the borders of what had become the republic of Austria but also those born in other parts of the monarchy. A similar procedure must have been used in classifying the immigrants' citizenship. Hence, for the years from 1925 to 1929, the lowest figure of 2,464, shown under "country of last permanent residence," should be taken as the most reliable indicator of the number of immigrants who can be considered to have been Austrians in the narrow sense of the word.

Owing to deteriorating economic conditions, rising unemployment and anti-immigration feeling, the total number of immigrants admitted to Canada first began to decline in 1930. Between 1931 and 1946, immigration levels fell sharply as a result of a 1931 order-in-council which restricted admissible classes of immigrants to British subjects,[9] U.S. Citizens, the wife and unmarried children under 18 and fiancé(e)s, and "agriculturalists having sufficient means to farm in Canada."[10] The total number of immigrants declined from 27,830 in 1931 to slightly over 10,000 in the years from 1933 to 1940, and to less than 10,000 during World War II.

Since persons residing outside Great Britain and Ireland were no longer admissible, the number of immigrants who could in one way or another be classified as "Austrian" also declined sharply during this period. In 1930, 663 persons were classified as Austrian citizens and 727 persons as having been born in Austria. Between 1931 and 1938 their numbers drop to 334 in the former and 503 in the latter category; during World War II, except for two Austrian citizens in 1939, only 258 persons born in Austria were accepted. Thus, the definitional problem as to who should be considered to be "Austrian" is similar to that applying to the 1925 and 1929 period. It is likely that country of birth again included the Austrian-Hungarian Monarchy while citizenship may have been more narrowly defined as including only those who were citizens of the republic.

## POST-WORLD WAR II IMMIGRATION POLICY

In 1946, one year after World War II had ended, the order-in-council of 1931 with its restrictions of classes of admissible immigrants, was still in force but, due to an acute shortage of labour in Canada's primary industries, farm workers, miners, and loggers were added.[11] It was only in May of 1947 that Mackenzie King, then prime minister of Canada, issued his by now famous statement on immigration policy which for the first time specified the criteria which were to guide the admission of immigrants. Within the limits of Canada's absorptive capacity of immigrants, immigration policy was to be guided by demographic considerations and the requirements of economic development. Even though the government recognized the need for immigrants, the door was still only open for European immigrants. As Mackenzie King further stated, in order not to alter the character of the Canadian population, the government was "opposed to large-scale immigration from the Orient" and had "no intention of changing the regulation governing Asian immigration unless and until alternative measures of effective control have been worked out."[12] The importance which the Canadian government attached to immigration was further underlined by the transfer in 1950 of the Immigration

Branch from the Department of Mines of Resources into a new Department of Citizenship and Immigration.

Although total immigration to Canada began to increase in 1946, the impact of the new policy was not immediately felt. With the exception of 1948, yearly total immigration did not exceed 100,000 until the end of the decade. A similar pattern holds for Austrian immigration, despite the fact that in 1948 the designation of Austrians as enemy aliens was removed and that in 1949 the first Canadian Immigration Office was opened in Salzburg. Between 1946 and 1950, the number of immigrants classified as Austrian citizens came to 992 but the number of those born in Austria reached 3,454, indicating again that the latter category must have included the territory of the former Austrian-Hungarian Empire.

AUSTRIAN IMMIGRATION FROM 1951 TO THE PRESENT

Immigration to Canada began to increase sharply as a result of a 1950 order-in-council which broadened the admissible classes of immigrants to include any immigrant "who satisfies the Minister that he is a suitable immigrant having regard to the climatic, the social, educational, labour or other conditions or requirements of Canada,"[13] but which retained in a more subtle language the exclusion of non-Europeans.[14] Between 1951 and 1960, with some fluctuations, the total number of yearly immigrants ranged between 150,000 and 190,000, with the exception of 1957, when about 280,000 persons arrived.

Austrian immigration also began to increase sharply in 1951, remained high until about 1954 but levelled off during the remaining years of the decade. Indeed, because of the large number of persons who entered during this period, the 1950s can be regarded as the prime decade of Austrian immigration, though we believe that our examination of immigration statistics does reveal a lower total number than is traditionally suggested. Between 1951 and 1954, the total number of Austrian citizens immigrating to Canada was 15,316 and the total number of immigrants born in Austria came to 15,717.

However, the picture becomes rather complicated for the remaining years of the decade. For the years from 1953 to 1966, immigrants who identified themselves as Austrians were no longer included among "Germans" but shown separately, and in 1955 the category Austria as a country of last residence was also re-introduced. In contradistinction to citizenship, country of birth or last residence, ethnic origin is not based on documentary evidence but on the immigrant's self-identification and should, therefore, be taken as the most reliable indicator of who should be considered an "Austrian." Indeed between 1953 and 1960, depending on which figure is taken, the number of immigrants who identified themselves as Austrians, was 17,171 or 17,428 but the number of immigrants who were Austrian citizens or born in Austria, with 19,541 and 19,468 respectively, was higher. Thus, although during this decade 26,036 immigrants were recorded as Austrian citizens, it is safe to assume that of these only between 23,000 and 24,000 were ethnic Austrians, that is, immigrants who identified themselves as such.

The discrepancies in the figures between "country of last residence," "country of citizenship" and "ethnic origin" in particular show that during the 1950s Austria has become a transit country for citizens of other countries who wished to immigrate to Canada. Of the 21,007 immigrants who gave Austria as their last country of residence between 1956 and 1960, apart from 7,847 ethnic Austrians, the largest numbers identified themselves as Yugoslavs, followed by Germans and Hungarians.[15]

Although over-all yearly immigration levels remained high throughout the 1960s, compared to the previous decade, considerably fewer Austrian citizens immigrated to Canada between 1961 and 1970 than did during the preceding decade; in total, 6,101 Austrian citizens immigrated to Canada during this period. However, the number of immigrants whose last country of residence was Austria came to 21,290. The difference between the two figures is mainly due to the inclusion of 8,501 immigrants with Czechoslovakian citizenship and smaller numbers of Yugoslavian and Hungarian citizens. Such a discrepancy again demonstrates Austria's importance as a transit country.

Levels of immigration remained high during the 1970s and most of the 1980s,[16] but Austrian immigration declined still further. Between 1971 and 1980 2,569 immigrants who were Austrian citizens and 2,855 immigrants who gave Austria as the country of birth were admitted to Canada; during the following decade the numbers decreased still further to 1,891 and 2,296 respectively. With the changing political climate, Austria's importance as a transit country similarly declined. Between 1971 and 1980, the number of immigrants who gave Austria as their last country of permanent residence dropped to 5,268; between 1981 and 1990 it fell to 2,220.

Several factors can be tentatively advanced in order to account for the decline in Austrian immigration during recent decades. Firstly, with economic opportunities available in Austria, migration no longer holds the same attraction as it did in the years following Word War II. Secondly, the 1962 immigration regulation removed any racial discrimination and established skills as the main criterion in the selection of economic immigrants, thus not only opening up immigration from non-European countries but increasing the competition of potential candidates with the required skills.[17] The impact of the regulations was not immediately felt, but since the mid-70s immigrants from third world countries have indeed consistently outnumbered immigrants from Europe. Thirdly, the 1976 Immigration Act further emphasized economic and labour power needs by introducing the point system. Since then, in order to be admitted, potential candidates must receive a certain minimum number of points which are awarded on the basis of several criteria, such as knowledge of one of Canada's official languages, educational attainment, and specific professional and vocational skills. The introduction of these criteria has probably further eroded the attractiveness of Canada as an immigration country for Austrians and Europeans generally, particularly if the skills recruited for Canada are in demand at home and emigration may mean the interruption of a promising career.

## THE CENSUS

As pointed out earlier, the census data provide what is usually called "stock" data, that is, periodic snapshots of a population and its characteristics. In Canada, census data are collected every 10 years, in calendar years ending in "1." The regular, decennial, data collection began in 1871, just after Confederation.[18] Since 1956, a quinquennial census has also been conducted. However, with the exception of the census of 1986, essentially a replication of the 1981 census, most of these quinquennial censuses are of limited use for our purposes. Canadian census data provide useful information for the study of ethnic groups. In general, data are available on the following characteristics:

*Ethnic origin*
    Data on ethnic origin of the Canadian population have been collected in all regular population censuses. The wording of the question has changed at various times.[19] Canadian census data on ethnic origin are strongly affected by several factors. These include, of course, the regular processes of demographic change, such as immigration of new group

members; emigration of persons belonging to a particular group; births and deaths. In addition, however, self-report data on ethnic origin and ancestry turn out to be affected by many other, external factors. The more salient ones are: changes in national boundaries, fluctuating acceptability of specific ethnic labels to members of the host society, lack of adequate information on the part of the census takers, and changes in data collection methodology. The Austrian-Canadian group has been affected strongly by several of these external factors. Not only did the country of origin go through major boundary changes after the end of the First World War but, as a consequence of the Second World War, various ethnic origin categories were also quite unpopular in Canadian society.[20]

### Place of birth

Since 1901, data on place of birth are available in all censuses. However, they have not been used extensively in analyses of specific ethnic groups in Canada. The data suffer clearly from the impact of boundary changes on the immigrants' country of origin as well. Thus, a precise understanding of the specifications by which these data were collected is important. As we shall see, respondents did not always understand these criteria and thus confused current boundaries and the boundaries which were operative at the time of their birth.

### Citizenship

As an "achieved" characteristic, citizenship is not as useful a criterion as the "ascribed" characteristics of ethnic origin and place of birth. In other words, in many societies, immigrants may lose their original citizenship when they become citizens of the new country by means of naturalization. Thus, when immigrants from Austria acquire Canadian citizenship by naturalization, they may lose their Austrian citizenship.

### Mother tongue

For many ethnic groups in Canada, additional information can be obtained by means of data on mother tongue, that is, the language first learned in early childhood and still understood. For groups such as Finnish-Canadians and Dutch-Canadians, such data are useful, since Finnish and, at least partially, Dutch, are monocentric languages (i.e., they are essentially spoken in one source country only). However, Austria shares the German language as standard language with Germany and Switzerland. Although there are obvious differences in the dialects used in these respective states and, moreover, minor differences in the standard languages as well, virtually all immigrants from Austria, defined by its post-World War I borders, will report having German as mother tongue. Some respondents to the census questions, especially as they were phrased through 1941, mentioned that they had "Austrian" as mother tongue.[21] However, some of these answers were obviously based either on the respondent's knowledge of a dialect or on a misunderstanding of the nature of languages. Generally, mother tongue responses of "Austrian" have been treated as equivalent to responses of German.

### ETHNIC ORIGIN IN THE CENSUSES OF THE PERIOD 1901-1991

In this section, summary information on Austrians, classified by ethnic origin, is provided as reported in the population censuses of 1901 through 1991. Table 2 shows the number of Austrians, defined in terms of ethnic origin, in the population censuses of 1901 through 1991 and, for purposes of comparison, the number of intercensal immigrants of Austrian citizenship, that is of Austrian citizens who immigrated to Canada during the period preceding the census year. Because of their different time frame, the immigration data in this table are, strictly speaking, not comparable to the census data. Since the immigration data reflect the total number of immigrant arrivals in periods such as 1901 through 1910 or 1961 through 1970, but the census is taken in the beginning of June in the years ending in "1," there is a slight slippage between the two sets of numbers. However, a quick inspection of the data in Table 2 shows that the slippage in dates is the least of the problems affecting these data.

In interpreting the data, several comments are in order. The first censuses, i.e., those for 1901 and 1911, were obviously affected by the multinational nature of the Austro-Hungarian Empire. Census takers, as well as those who designed the final published tabulations, were clearly aware of the fact that the Empire contained Austrians as well as Hungarians and, consequently, the published tables generally give frequencies for these two categories separately. However, they were not altogether cognizant of the existence of various other ethnic groups, such as Slovaks, Slovenians and Ukrainians. Such lack of clarity was gradually resolved; as a result, it is often possible to reconstruct the proper breakdown of these ethnic categories on the basis of retrospective tabulations published in more recent censuses. Based on these reconstructions, the frequency reported for 1901

did include persons of Austrian origin as well as of "Bukovinian origin."
For the 1901 census data, the latter category cannot be separated from the
total given. Since the 1911 census reported only 9,960 "Bukovinians,"
their number was probably much smaller in 1901.

Table 2. Population of Austrian ethnic origin, Canada, 1901-1991

| Year | ethnic origin | | intercensal immigration |
| | single | multiple | |
| --- | --- | --- | --- |
| 1901 | 10947 | n/a | n/a |
| 1911 | 42535 | n/a | 20155 |
| 1921 | 107671 | n/a | 9617 |
| 1931 | 48639 | n/a | 5486 |
| 1941 | 37715 | n/a | 336 |
| 1951 | 32231 | n/a | 992 |
| 1961 | 106535 | n/a | 26036 |
| 1971 | 42120 | n/a | 6686 |
| 1981 | 40630 | n/a | 2569 |
| 1986 | 24900 | 49735 | 848 |
| 1991 | 27130 | 66780 | 1043 |

A comparison of the census data for 1901, 1911 and 1921 with the
immigration data for the period 1900 through 1920 confirms our suspicion about the reliability and validity of the data in these censuses. Immigration statistics, in themselves of doubtful quality, show that 20,155
Austrian immigrants arrived in Canada in the period 1901 through 1910,
and 9,617 between 1911 and 1920, yet the 1911 and 1921 censuses give
the number of ethnic Austrians as 43,535 and 107,671 respectively. Thus,
differences in the census figures for the two decades are 31,588 and
65,136 respectively. Obviously, both the 1911 and the 1921 censuses
have severely inflated numbers of Austrians by ethnic origin. The extent
of the inflation of the numbers for 1921 is demonstrated very clearly by
the fact that in 1931 the number of Austrians, defined by ethnic origin,
had declined by 59,032 to 48,639!

An examination of more detailed data for 1921 and 1931, at the
level of provinces, shows that the provinces affected most strongly by the
decline were Manitoba, Saskatchewan and Alberta. As Table 3 shows, for
all three of these provinces, the number of respondents giving Austrian
as ethnic origin decreased markedly from 1921 to 1931. However, the

overall populations of these provinces did not decline in similar fashions. In other words, the precipitous drop in the number of persons with Austrian as ethnic origin between 1921 and 1931 is not likely to have resulted from massive emigration of such persons during that period. Patterns of this nature present us with puzzles of a peculiar form: they do not reflect "real" population processes, such as migration, fertility or mortality, but rather the social and cultural factors on the basis of which people identify themselves by ethnic origin or some other cultural characteristic. Indeed, an examination of other ethnic categories shows that, during this same period, the number of persons who identified themselves as "German," "Polish" and "Ukrainian" all increased by large numbers. Although it is not possible to establish what happened exactly during the period 1921-1931, it is apparent that social and cultural factors on the basis of which people identify themselves by ethnic origin or some other cultural characteristic contributed to changes in the respondents' ethnic self-identification.

*Table 3. Population of selected ethnic origins for Manitoba, Saskatchewan and Alberta, 1921 and 1931*

|  |  | Austrian | German | Polish | Ukrainian |
|---|---|---|---|---|---|
| Manitoba | 1921 | 31035 | 19444 | 16594 | 44129 |
|  | 1931 | 8858 | 38078 | 40243 | 73606 |
|  | difference | -22177 | 18634 | 23649 | 29477 |
| Saskatchewan | 1921 | 39738 | 68202 | 8161 | 28097 |
|  | 1931 | 17061 | 129232 | 25961 | 63400 |
|  | difference | -22677 | 61030 | 17800 | 35303 |
| Alberta | 1921 | 19430 | 35333 | 7172 | 23827 |
|  | 1931 | 6737 | 74450 | 21157 | 55872 |
|  | difference | -12693 | 39117 | 13985 | 32045 |

Relative to 1931, the 1941 census data show a further decline in the number of "ethnic" Austrians. Even the reduced numbers turn out, on closer inspection, to be inflated. In this census, the ethnic data on Austrians were strongly affected by the Second World War, as well as by the already noted multinational and multilingual nature of the Austro-

Hungarian Empire. Hurd provides a thoughtful discussion of the complex issues involved in self-identification by ethnic origin, in the 1941 census monograph on *Ethnic Origin and Nativity of the Canadian People.*[22] As Hurd notes, of the 37,715 persons who reported Austrian as ethnic origin, 17 percent gave Ukrainian as mother tongue, "yet there was very little Ukrainian spoken within the boundaries of Austria as determined by the Treaty of Versailles."[23] In addition, Hurd suspects that data on Austria as place of birth are similarly affected. Some respondents also reported "Austrian" as mother tongue. The 1941 monograph states "Since there is no Austrian language, such persons obviously were confused when answering the questions of the census enumerator—a circumstance which supports one's suspicion as to the accuracy of the total figure for the Austrian ethnic origin group. The evidence points to considerable overstatement."[24]

An additional factor which may have contributed to the inflation of the number of persons of Austrian ethnic origin in the 1941 census is the avoidance of the category "German." The 1941 monograph mentions the effect such avoidance had on the category "Dutch." In a journal article published shortly after the printing date of the 1941 census monograph, Ryder shows that "Austrian" was also a convenient substitute for "German." It will not be possible to estimate the exact extent of this inflation. According to Hurd's estimates, the Ukrainian component by itself may have amounted to 17 percent of the total number of ethnic Austrians, or to about 6,500 persons. The detailed data in Table 1 in the 1941 census monograph suggest that there may be an additional 3,000 persons (with mother tongues such as Italian, Romanian, Magyar, Bohemian, Slovak, Polish, Russian and Serbo-Croatian) whose somewhat confused responses contributed to the inflation of the 1941 data on ethnic "Austrians." However, the magnitude of the inflation due to avoidance of "German" cannot be estimated with any degree of accuracy.

Given the previous numbers, the 1951 data appear reasonable, although they may still be somewhat inflated. They are also consistent with the data on Austria as country of birth, as can be seen by an inspection of Table 4. However, the next puzzle occurs in 1961, for which the data are as suspect as the ones for 1921. The increase from 1951 to 1961 involves over 70,000 persons. One may be tempted to attribute this increase to massive immigration during the 1950s; the available evidence does not support this hypothesis.

*Table 4. Population born in Austria, Canada, 1901-1991*

| 1901 | 28407 |
|------|-------|
| 1911 | 67502 |
| 1921 | 57535 |
| 1931 | 37391 |
| 1941 | 50713 |
| 1951 | 37598 |
| 1961 | 70192 |
| 1971 | 40450 |
| 1981 | 34325 |
| 1986 | 30635 |
| 1991 | 26680 |

Tabulations in the 1961 census (Bulletin 7.1-7, table 6) show that there were 21,013 persons, born in Austria, who immigrated to Canada in the period 1951-1961. Since, based on the immigration statistics we discussed earlier, it was estimated that 23,000 to 24,000 Austrians (defined by ethnic origin) immigrated to Canada during this period, it is probable that the 21,013 persons born in Austria include only those who also identified themselves as Austrian. Thus, depending on which figure is accepted, the number of persons born in Austria would have increased from 32,231 in 1951 to only 53,244 or to between 54,000 and 55,000 in 1961. This would still leave between 51,000 and 53,000 persons, or about half of the "ethnic Austrians" in 1961 unaccounted for!

In 1971, the total number of persons reporting Austrian as ethnic origin declined markedly from its inflated value in 1961. Without further analysis, it is not clear how these enormous discrepancies of a pronounced increase in one decade followed by an equally pronounced decrease in the next decade could be explained. However, a detailed demographic analysis of census data on Ukrainians by de Vries suggests that a large fraction of these discrepancies, reported above, may have involved differential propensities for respondents to label themselves as "Austrian" by ethnic origin. In a mirror image to the Austrian data, the Ukrainian data showed an inexplicably large increase from 1961 to 1971, which could not be explained in terms of normal demographic processes of birth, death and migration; detailed analyses by five-year birth cohorts suggested that the period 1961-1971 saw a shift in self-identification, from Austrian ethnic origin in 1961 to Ukrainian ethnic origin in 1971. This shift affected all age-groups and contributed to the (apparent) decline in the number of ethnic Austrians between 1961 and 1971.[25]

Much of this pattern of contrasting trends may in fact be due to two major changes in data collection. In the first place, the 1971 census shifted from an enumeration procedure to a "drop-off mail-back" procedure. Thus, there was no longer an enumerator sitting across from the respondent; the resulting privacy may have allowed many persons to give answers they might not have given previously. It is not possible to assess the impact of this change on the tendency to report specific ethnic origins, correctly or incorrectly.

A second change in data collection procedures may also have contributed to the drastic decline in the number of ethnic Austrians between 1961 and 1971. In 1961, the census form provided 28 specific ethnic categories in alphabetical order. Of these 28, Austrian was the first one listed. It is conceivable that many respondents who had one or more Austrian ancestors marked the Austrian category, as the first applicable one on a long list. In 1971, however, the census form listed only 13 categories, but these categories did not include Austrian ethnic origin by name. In other words, persons who wanted to identify themselves as Austrian had to use the "write-in" category to report their ethnic identification. Kralt suggests that these changes in layout contributed strongly to the sometimes very large swings in ethnic group frequencies between 1961 and 1971.[26] While it is tempting to accept this explanation, other factors have to be considered as well, as we shall see further on in this paper.

The 1981 census introduced yet another change in the data collection procedures. Until, and including, 1971, the question on ethnic origin had always referred to the respondent's ancestry on the male side. Thus, persons whose parents did not belong to the same ethnic group ended up reporting only the origin of their father—or of the foreign-born ancestor in the paternal line—while the mother's ethnic origin remained hidden, as it were. Since the 1981 data omitted, for the first time, any mention of the "male side," respondents could give more than one response. The census forms and instruction booklets did not inform respondents that multiple responses were permitted; White and her colleagues indicate that, nevertheless, 11 percent of the total Canadian population gave multiple responses.[27] These multiple responses were edited to single ones by rather complex and poorly documented editing procedures. It would be quite conceivable, therefore, that a non-trivial proportion of the 40,630 responses in 1981 were originally multiple responses of "Austrian" and some other category.

The censuses of 1986 and 1991 not only allowed multiple responses, but respondents were specifically informed that multiple responses were permitted, by means of the phrase "Mark or specify as many as applicable." In both censuses, 28 percent of the total Canadian population gave more than one response to the question on ethnic origin.[28]

As can be seen in Table 2, the census data for 1986 and 1991 are split into two separate categories: the first column reports the number of persons who gave a single response of "Austrian," while the second column gives the number of people who gave multiple responses which included "Austrian." Given the ratio between the two sets of figures (the number of multiple responses is more than twice that of the number of single responses), it is likely that many of the 40,630 in 1981 were also of mixed ethnic ancestry. Note that the percentages of Austrian-Canadians who gave multiple responses in 1986 and 1991 were well above the total value of 28 percent reported above!

It is important to point out that, according to the immigration statistics, from 1951 to 1990 37,182 persons came to Canada who were Austrian citizens, but the 1991 census lists only 27,130 persons who gave "Austrian" as a single response to the ethnic origin question, while another 66,780 counted at least one Austrian among their ancestors. Since some of the immigrant Austrian citizens undoubtedly returned to their home country, while others may have moved to the United States, and since the census also includes ethnic "Austrians" who were born in Canada, we would expect that immigration figures would be different from those in the census. However, the fact that the number of "ethnic Austrians" declines steadily in the post-war period suggests that the immigrants and their descendants have successfully integrated into Canada's multicultural society.

### COUNTRY OF BIRTH FOR THE PERIOD 1901-1991

Data on the country of birth, summarized in Table 4, tell a story not all that different from those on ethnic origin in Table 2. We should note that the figure for 1901, of 28,407, pertains to Austria-Hungary. Given the political structure of Central and Eastern Europe during that era, it is highly probable that many of the 28,407 were born in parts of the Empire in which Austrian had little or no relation to language, ethnicity or culture. Similar comments may be made on the data for 1911 and 1921, and probably for several of the subsequent censuses as well, even though data from 1911 onward do not include those born in Hungary.

It is likely that the pronounced increase from 1901 to 1911 indeed reflects large numbers of immigrants from different parts of the Empire; as we pointed out in a prior section of this paper, the immigration data for that decade are well below the intercensal increase shown in Table 4. Obviously, the 1911 census data on Austria as country of birth are somewhat inflated. The data for 1921 present a puzzle: in contradistinction to the enormous increase in the numbers of people reporting Austrian as ethnic origin, the data on country of birth show a small decrease! Perhaps the historians have an explanation of what happened here. Avoidance of Austria as place of birth appears to be inconsistent with the accompanying rise in popularity of Austrian ethnic origin.

The drop between 1921 and 1931 is, on the other hand, consistent with the decline we saw in the ethnic origin data. The data for 1941 show contrasting patterns—Austrian ethnic origin becomes less popular than it was in 1931; at the same time, Austria as country of birth becomes more popular. Table 1 in the 1941 census monograph suggests that a large number of those born in Austria were, in fact, Ukrainian in ethnic origin.

The data on place of birth for 1951 look credible. Yet the 1961 data show a similar, though less pronounced, inflation as that for the ethnic origin data, noted earlier. The number of persons who gave Austria as place of birth data increased by about 33,000—an increase which can, again, not be explained by large volumes of immigration during the period 1951 through 1961. Based on immigration statistics, the best estimate of the number of immigrants, born in Austria, arriving in Canada between 1951 and 1961 is about 26,700. When we consider that not all of the people who immigrated between 1951 and 1961 would be counted in the 1961 census, it becomes apparent that the 1961 census data on place of birth are overestimates, though clearly not to the same extent as the ethnic origin data were.

The notion that the 1961 data on place of birth were inflated is further supported by the drastic decline between 1961 and 1971, from 70,192 to 40,450, in the number of persons who reported that they were born in Austria. It should also be noted that the 1971 data on ethnic origin and on place of birth are closer to each other than they were in any of the preceding census years. That observation should not be taken as a strong verification of either one of the two figures, however. Based on a strict reading of the census question, ethnic origin is a characteristic which one inherits at birth, but which does not require a respondent to be born outside Canada. In contrast, place of birth outside Canada is not passed on to the next generation. In other words, the data on ethnic origin should contain a sizeable proportion born in Canada, especially for an ethnic group such as the Austrian one, which has a long residence history in Canada. Thus, we would expect the number of Austrians by ethnic origin to be considerably larger than the number of persons born in Austria. This relation is indeed observable in the data for 1981 and the following decade. In this context it is important to point out, again, that the 1981 data on ethnic origin were the result of an editing process in which an unknown number of persons with multiple ethnic origins composed of "Austrian" and some other category ended up as "Austrian," whereas other respondents with multiple ethnic origins ended up with a label other than "Austrian." In contrast, all multiple responses containing Austrian in the 1986 and 1991 censuses were included in the "multiples" column. Thus, the data on country of birth for 1986 and 1991 look credible, given what we know about immigration data and about the age structure of the Austrian-Canadian population.

In this paper, we have examined data on Austrians in Canada, both with regards to the flows of international migrants into the country and with regards to the periodic inventories taken in the decennial and quinquennial censuses of population. We have shown that, for most of the period 1901 through 1991, these data give an inflated picture of the number of "true" Austrians, that is, those Canadians who, either through ethnic identification or through their country of birth, have a connection to the present Republic of Austria. While the magnitude of this inflation has declined since 1961, it is not possible to state with any degree of certainty whether the most recent figures are still inflated or whether they are telling the "true" story. The picture which emerges for the last decade of the century suggests that Austrian immigrants and their descendants have intermarried with other Canadians to a significant extent (as witnessed by the large number of persons who reported having multiple ethnic origins, of which Austrian was one). Such patterns of intermarriage are consistent with the notion that Austrian immigrants have, generally, integrated successfully into Canadian society.

ENDNOTES

1. The regular decennial data collection began in 1871, i.e., just after Confederation. Prior to 1871, several of the components of Canada had conducted population censuses; the earliest one on record was Jean Talon's census of 1665 in Nouveau France. See Warren Kalbach and Wayne McVey, *The Demographic Bases of Canadian Society* (Toronto, 1971), pp. 1-9 for a detailed description of Canadian census practices.

2. The British Colonial Office was responsible for establishing and administering immigration policy for British North America. Cf. Gerald E. Dirks, *Canada's Refugee Policy: Indifference or Opportunism?* (Montreal and London, 1977), p. 25.

3. With the passage of the British North America Act in 1867, the responsibility for immigration was assigned to provincial and federal authorities. In 1872 Ottawa assumed full responsibility for the formulation of the policy and the admission of immigrants. Dirks, *ibid.*, p. 25.

4. Daniel Kubat, ed., *The Politics of Migration Policies* (New York, 1993), pp. 26-27. Despite the heavy emphasis on attracting agricultural settlers, John Porter, citing occupational statistics, has shown that in 1871 only about half of the labour force were farmers, lumbermen and fishermen. The downward trend continued even during the period of massive migration. The proportion of rural population declined from 80.4 percent in 1871, to 62.5 percent in 1901 and 54.6 percent 1911. John Porter, *The Vertical Mosaic: An Analysis of Social Class and Power in Canada* (Toronto, 1965), pp. 136-39.

5. *Ibid.*, p. 27.

6. Freda Hawkins, *Canada and Immigration: Public Policy and Public Concern* (Montreal, 1972), p. 402.

7. Kubat, *Migration Policies*, p. 27.

8. Dirks, *Refugee Policy*, pp. 37-41.

9. British subjects were defined by a previous order of council as "British by reason of birth, or naturalization in Great Britain or Ireland, Newfoundland, New Zealand, Australia and the Union of South Africa." Hawkins, *Canada and Immigration* p. 90.

10. *Ibid.,* pp. 89-90; Dirks, *Refugee Policy*, p. 42.

11. Hawkins, *Canada and Immigration*, p. 91.

12. *Ibid.*, p. 93.

13. *Ibid.*, p. 99.

14. The order-in-council further stipulated that any immigrant is admissible who "is not undesirable owing to his probable inability to become readily adapted and

integrated into the life of the Canadian community and to assume the duties of Canadian citizenship within a reasonable time after his entry" *(Ibid.,* p. 99).

15. This figure does not include the 37,565 Hungarian refugees who had fled to Austria and were resettled in Canada.

16. However, with the large-scale admission of Southeast Asian refugees between 1979 and 1981 the composition of immigrants also began to change significantly. As a result of the recession in the 1980s, immigration levels fell below the 100,000 level and the majority of immigrants were admitted as family class members and refugees.

17. The importance of economic considerations in the formulation of immigration policy was underlined by the removal in 1966 of Immigration from Citizenship and the creation of the Department of Manpower and Immigration.

18. Cf. endnote 1, above.

19. See Pamela M. White, et al., "Measuring ethnicity in Canadian censuses," in Gustave J. Goldmann and Nampeo R. McKenney, eds., *Challenges of Measuring an Ethnic World: Science, Politics and Reality. Proceedings of the Joint Canada-United States Conference on the Measurement of Ethnicity* (Washington, 1993), pp. 223-69, for a detailed description of past practices.

20. A detailed analysis of this phenomenon has been provided by Norman B. Ryder, "The interpretation of origin statistics," *Canadian Journal of Economics and Political Science,* 21 (1955), 466-79.

21. See, for example, Burton Hurd, *Ethnic Origin and Nativity of the Canadian People* (1941 census monograph) (Ottawa, 1954), p. 130.

22. *Ibid.,* pp. 30-31 and Table 1 on pp. 191-93. Incidentally, the monograph was never publicly released.

23. *Ibid.,* p. 30.

24. *Ibid.*

25. John de Vries, "Explorations in the demography of language and ethnicity: The case of Ukrainians in Canada," in Tova Yedlin, ed., *Central and East European Ethnicity in Canada: Adaptation and Preservation* (Edmonton, 1985), pp. 130-31.

26. John Kralt, *Profile Studies: Ethnic Origins of Canadians* (Ottawa, 1977).

27. White, et al., "Measuring Ethnicity," pp. 223-69.

28. *Ibid.,* p. 230.

III

# PUSH AND PULL FACTORS FOR OVERSEAS MIGRANTS FROM AUSTRIA-HUNGARY IN THE 19ᵀᴴ AND 20ᵀᴴ CENTURIES

*Michael John*
*University of Linz*

THE TRANSITION FROM PREINDUSTRIAL to industrial social structures is inseparably linked with the mobilization of manpower. Millions were set in motion by this process, migrating from rural areas into the cities, between urban centers, across national boundaries and overseas. The direction of migration, however, was always from economically less advanced to more highly developed regions. Overseas emigration on a broad scale began comparatively late in Austria-Hungary, where the necessary preconditions for such mass migratory movements—freedom of travel, cheap means of mass transportation and adequate methods of informational exchange concerning the labor and living conditions in the destination countries—were relatively slow in developing.

## THE QUANTITATIVE DEVELOPMENT OF EMIGRATION

Emigration out of Austria-Hungary developed along clearly divergent paths in the two halves of the Dual Monarchy, among its various regions and ethnic groups and during different phases of economic development. The first records providing a systematic statistical picture of emigration date from the year 1819. Until the 1850s, emigration was rather limited —from 1821 to 1830, 14,255 Habsburg subjects left the Austrian provinces of the empire for destinations overseas; between 1831 and 1840, the total was 7,536. Data is missing for several years during the 1840s so that the time series cannot be compiled for this period. In the decade 1851-1860, the number of emigrants climbed to 27,045. Finally, from 1861 until 1866, the last year before the proclamation of the Dual Monarchy, emigration totaled 14,693 persons.[1]

A completely unrestricted right to emigrate did not exist in Austria at that time. Those wishing to emigrate legally had to petition formally for that right; those receiving authorization lost their "status as Austrian subjects" and were subsequently treated as foreigners. The motivating factors in this early phase were of an economic, political and religious nature. Politically motivated emigration was one of many manifestations which marked the *Vormärz* period leading up to the Revolution of 1848, when critical intellectuals regarded the overseas option in a comparatively liberal and vibrant U.S.A. as significantly more attractive than the repressive regime of Count Metternich.[2] Austrian revolutionaries also fled to the United States in 1848 and the year thereafter. Finally, during the crisis of the 1850s, a certain percentage of the rural population emigrated for economic reasons. It is by no means surprising, however, that among them were a great number of Protestants motivated by the fear that Neoabsolutism would bring with it a diminished tolerance toward their religious confessions. This wave of emigration affected mainly the provinces of Upper Austria (especially the Salzkammergut region),[3] Carinthia and Tyrol. During the 1860s, emigration from the western provinces sank to virtually zero; throughout this period, Bohemia was the region showing by far the most emigration.[4]

The *Staatsgesetz* of 1867 proclaimed the right of the individual to emigrate: "At present in Austria, the freedom of emigration is restricted only by the duty of military service."[5] Despite the fact that certain discrepancies are evident in the data available from state archival sources, it is nevertheless possible from this time on to observe the development of overseas emigration out of the Austrian (or so-called Cisleithatian) half of the empire on a year by year basis. It was only in the 1890s and, above all, in the period after the turn of the century, that emigration first achieved truly significant proportions: from 1867 to 1913, 2,394,796 overseas emigrants left the Austrian half of the empire, of whom 1,588,747 or 66.3 percent did so in the period between 1900 and 1913. Thus, emigration reached an especially high level during the early part of the 20th century, experiencing only a temporary decline connected with a severe business cycle downturn in the United States between the years of 1908 and 1911. The United States was the destination of the majority of emigrants.

Graph 1.   *Emigration from the Austrian Half of the Austro-Hungarian Empire, 1867-1913*

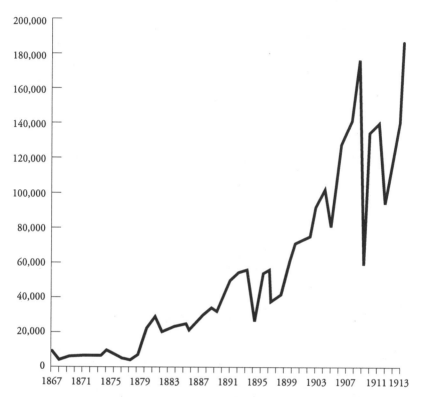

*Source:* Birgit Bolognese-Leuchtenmüller, *Bevölkerungsentwicklung und Berufsstruktur, Gesundheits- und Fürsorgewesen in Österreich 1750-1918* (Vienna, 1978), pp. 131-37.

Based upon an analysis of emigration from 1876 to 1910 by destination country, we know that 1,531,382 Austrians, or 83 percent of all Austrian emigrants, emigrated to the United States of America, 151,913 or 8.2 percent to Canada, 94,047 or 5.1 percent to Argentina and 55,860 or 3 percent to Brazil. Canada's share increased to 15-18 percent between the years 1911 and 1913. The most immediately noticeable divergent trend displayed by the Hungarian half of the empire in comparison to Austria was that the proportion of emigration to Canada was virtually insignificant while emigration to Argentina accounted for 15.5

percent and was thus proportionately much higher. The absolute number of emigrants from the two halves of the empire was nearly the same (Austria 1,845,382, Hungary 1,702,248) though, as a result of Austria's higher population, the proportion of its total number of inhabitants who emigrated was lower than in Hungary (Austria 6.5 percent, Hungary 8.1 percent).

The census of 1910 shows that internal migration (i.e. between political districts within the Monarchy) was approximately three times larger than overseas emigration, while the number of new immigrants into Austria-Hungary covered only a quarter of the population lost to emigration abroad.

*Table 1.   The Transcontinental Migration from Austria-Hungary by Destination Land 1876-1910. (Based on official statistics)*

|                              | Austria   | Hungary   |
| ---------------------------- | --------- | --------- |
| USA                          | 1,531,382 | 1,422,205 |
| Canada                       | 151,913   | 6,056     |
| Argentina                    | 94,047    | 264,460   |
| Brazil                       | 55,860    | 8,500     |
| other South American states  | 6,285     | 259       |
| Africa                       | 1,185     | 586       |
| Australia                    | 3,919     | 178       |
| Asia                         | 105       | 4         |
| Unknown                      | 686       | 0         |
| Total                        | 1,845,382 | 1,702,248 |

*Source:* Karl Ritter von Englisch, "Die österreichische Auswanderungsstatistik," *Statistische Monatsschrift,* Neue Folge 18 (1913), 73.

The fact that mass-scale emigration out of northern Europe (most notably Sweden), Germany and Great Britain took place significantly earlier than in Austria-Hungary is an indicator of this far-flung central European empire's deliberate orientation toward economic autarky and of the fact that its integration into the international labor market occurred significantly later than in those countries named above. Great Britain and

Germany, whose economies were already very highly developed around the turn of the century, were the lands of origin of markedly fewer emigrants during this period than was Austria-Hungary. With respect to immigration into the United States during the period 1902-1911, the Dual Monarchy led all nations with 27.9 percent of the total, followed by Italy with 26.6 percent, Russia with 21.3 percent, Great Britain with 11.8 percent, Sweden with 5.8 percent and Germany with 4.5 percent.[6] In the Canadian case, Austria-Hungary, as the land of origin of 7.3 percent of all immigrants, took third place behind Great Britain (38.7 percent) and the USA (34.2 percent) and followed by Russia (5.1 percent), Italy (3.3 percent) and Germany (1.3 percent).[7]

*Table 2.    Migration in the Monarchy: Internal Migration, Overseas Emigration and Immigration, 1910*

| Population | Internal Migration Political districts | Overseas Emigration | Immigration | Total |
|---|---|---|---|---|
| Cisleithania | 28.571.934 | 6.350.000 | 1.845.000 | 632.000 |
| Transleithania | 20.886.487 | 3.006.000 | 1.702.000 | 277.000 |
| Total | 49.458.421 | 9.356.000 | 3.547.000 | 909.000 |

*Source:* Heinz Fassmann, "Emigration, Immigration and Internal Migration," in Dirk Hoerder and Inge Blank, eds., *Roots of the Transplanted* (New York, 1994) vol. 1, 276.

## ON THE ETHNIC MAKE-UP AND SOCIAL STRUCTURE OF EMIGRANTS

The somewhat unsatisfactory statistical material on the occupational structure of Austrian emigrants from 1876 to 1910 displays a clear dominance of the agricultural professions with 45.4 percent of all emigrants, followed by craftsmen and industrial workers with 8.9 percent, and 2.8 percent engaged in commerce and trade; 21.7 percent were simply recorded as "labourers" without further specification. As a blanket generalization applicable to this entire period, though especially valid for the time around the turn of the century, it may be broadly asserted that the group of emigrants was typically made up of the impoverished and occupationally unskilled rural population of the territories in the north-east, east and southeast. More precise data is available for the years 1901-1910 with respect to emigration from the entire Austro-Hungarian Monarchy to the United States, which indeed shows a slightly smaller though still considerable proportion of agricultural laborers. Conversely, the percentage of those working in the productive and service sectors had already begun to rise by that time, with the figures showing 15.9 percent craftsmen and tradesmen, 23.8 percent day laborers, 10.2 percent domestic servants and 19.5 percent agricultural workers (see Graph 2). During the final years before the outbreak of the First World War, immigration into the United States was going through a clear process of restructuring, as evidenced by the distinct and continuous drop in the proportion of agricultural workers. At the same time, statistics show an increase in immigration to Canada by Austro-Hungarian citizens, among whom workers in the agricultural sector were very clearly predominant. We also have available data concerning age and gender for emigrants to the United States: according to this material, two thirds of the emigrants were men and 82 percent were in their prime productive years between the ages of 14 and 45.[8]

We have information concerning the ethnic make-up of the emigrant population—not from the Austrian statistical sources but rather from the American. Within the Austrian half of the Empire, the German-speaking population was strongly underrepresented among emigrants; likewise, in the Hungarian half, Hungarian-speakers were underrepresented while the Slavic population was markedly overrepresented among the emigrants. In the Dual Monarchy during the period from 1901 to 1910, 18.6 percent of the emigrants were Poles, 16.1 percent were Serbs, Croats and Slovenes, 15.4 percent Slovaks, 14.7 percent Magyars and 11.8 percent Germans. The American statistical material treated Jews as a separate ethnic group; according to these figures, 7.1 percent of the Austro-Hungarian emigrants were Jews. The balance was made up of other groups such as Ukrainians, Czechs, and Romanians (see Graph 3). Regions which contributed large numbers of emigrants were Galicia and Bukovina, the Slovakian-speaking parts of Hungary, along with central and eastern Hungary and the southeastern portion of the Monarchy (Croatia, Slovenia and parts of Bosnia). This indicates that the areas of the empire which lay within the current borders of Austria were not among those regions with a high proportion of emigration.

*Graph 2.  Occupational Structure of Emigration to the U.S. from the Monarchy, 1901-1910*

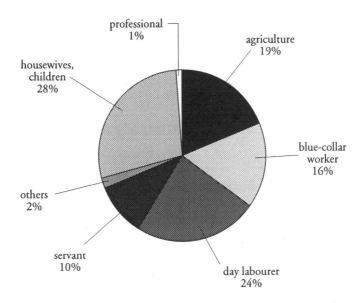

*Source:* Ernö Deak, "Die Auswanderung—eine Massenbewegung," in *Das Zeitalter Kaiser Franz Josephs,* Part 2: *1880-1916—Glanz und Elend: Beiträge* (Vienna, 1987), p. 34.

When using the borbers of modern-day Austria as a framework, the individual emigration patters become quite clear. Despite the unavailability of exact statistics, this process can be reconstructed and inferences can be drawn which suggest the motives for emigration. The region of modern Burgenland must be mentioned at the top of this list. The easternmost province of present-day Austria was then the westernmost portion of the Hungarian half of the empire (Districts of Moson, Sopron and Vas); the majority of the inhabitants spoke German, there was a large Croatian-speaking population as well as a smaller group who spoke exclusively Hungarian. Germans and Croats were thus in the position of minorities—vulnerable to the assimilation efforts of the Hungarian authorities, who also showed little interest in industrialization measures or infrastructure improvements in a border region with a strong minority contingent. The strongest emigration movement occurred in the county of Vas (Eisenburg) in what is today South Burgenland, though it was also quite considerable in Moson (Wieselburg) and Sopron (Ödenburg) counties. A calculation based upon Hungarian statistics shows that, prior to 1914, at least 26,000 emigrants, representing 13 percent of the entire population, left this region.[9]

*Graph 3. National Composition of Austro-Hungarian Overseas Emigration (to the U.S.) 1901-1910*

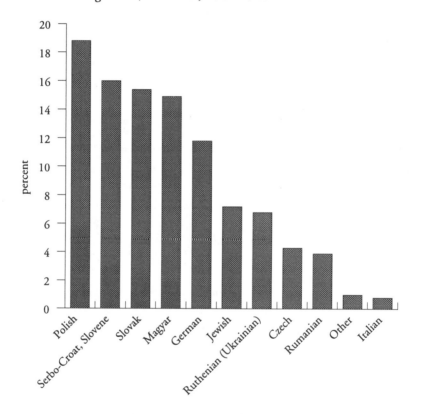

*Source:* Ernö Deak, "Die Auswanderung—eine Massenbewegung," in *Das Zeitalter Kaiser Franz Josephs,* Part 2: *1880-1916—Glanz und Elend: Beiträge* (Vienna, 1987), p. 33.

Narrowing the focus of inquiry to the final years before the outbreak of World War I reveals this period to have been one of atypical development in comparison to the time before 1910. In the fiscal years 1910-11, 1911-12 and 1912-13, a total of 20,701 German-speakers emigrated overseas from the Austrian half of the empire, along with 26,690 Bohemians (Czechs) and 30,467 Jews.[10] Since the census of 1910 indicates that the crown lands of Bohemia and Galicia showed by no means unusually high rates of emigration, while Lower Austria and Vienna displayed by far the highest figures (five times that of Bohemia, six times more than Galicia), and keeping in mind that a great many Jews and Czechs lived in Vienna and the neighboring environs of Lower Austria, it is certainly reasonable to assume that a portion of these minorities numbered among the emigrants. It is, after all, well documented by original census data that many emigrants lived for years in Vienna before making the decision to emigrate abroad. A few other examples of emigration from the territory of modern-day Austria worth mentioning are groups from Styria and especially from the multi-lingual region in southern Styria (much of which is actually in present day Slovenia) as well as those from Tyrol and Vorarlberg on the far western edge of the Monarchy. On the other hand, emigration from Upper Austria, Salzburg and Carinthia were quantitatively quite limited and comparatively irrelevant.

## PUSH AND PULL FACTORS:
### THE MOTIVES FOR EMIGRATION ABROAD

The model of push and pull forces is today the most frequently employed migration theory. According to this approach, an individual's decision to migrate is reached under the influence of so-called push and pull forces (repulsion and attraction). The decision making process is envisioned as a field of tension in which a variety of factors interact. We can specify four different groups of preconditions which govern the emigration process: factors connected with the region of origin; factors connected with the destination region; intervening hindrances (e.g. emigration laws, transportation costs, etc.); and personal factors (e.g. age, intelligence, military service etc.).[11] The reason which leads a human being to forsake his or her place of birth is just as likely to be the hopelessness of continuing to eke out a meager existence in an environment in which the conditions of life have sunk to the very margin of subsistence, as it is to be the hope of enjoying a better standard of life, and even moving up the social ladder, in another region or another land. Impoverishment, overpopulation and looming unemployment are classic examples of push factors which have provided motivation for emigration from rural areas. Pull factors are, for example, a well-functioning labor market, better occupational training and chances for advancement as well as a higher salary level. These classic push and pull factors play a dominant role in Austrian emigration abroad.

*Push factors*

Following the Revolution of 1848, capitalism began to make inroads into an Austrian agricultural system which still continued to display signs of its feudal past. One result of this development was dependence on market forces which had drastic consequences in the 1880s in the form of a steep drop in grain and sugar prices. The number of forced auctions of farm properties reached record levels not only during the years 1878-1892 but again during a protracted phase of depressed prices in 1900-1910. An additional structural change during this period can be identified in the growth of the number of small farms. These small agricultural operations were barely capable of feeding their proprietors and forced them into side-line work. Finally, there was also farm labor unemployment resulting from a certain degree of mechanization in the agricultural sector in the second half of the 19th century. The absence of chances to earn a living, impoverishment and pauperization in agrarian regions were thus significant push factors for all types of migration including emigration.[12] The number of middle-size farms had declined as a result of subdividing, itself a consequence of overpopulation. In vast portions of Hungary and in Galicia, the land was extremely unequally distributed—on the one hand, there existed large latifundia; on the other, masses of unskilled agricultural laborers working for extremely low pay.[13] Leopold Caro, speaking on behalf of the Businessmen's Association, described the situation in 1909 as follows: "The widespread latifundia, the absence of good-paying jobs here at home, nonexistent or minimal development of domestic industry and the low level of public education may well be considered the main causes of emigration throughout Austria."[14] In general, the economic situation in the northeastern and southeastern crown lands and regions of Austria and Hungary can be described as ones of increasing economic polarization within the Monarchy, economic differences were becoming more profound.

Demographic pressure as a result of relative overpopulation in agrarian regions was an additional essential push factor. In the second half of the nineteenth century up to the outbreak of the First World War, we may properly speak of a tendency in many regions toward virtual depopulation, referred to in contemporary accounts as a "general flight from the land."[15] In many agrarian regions, the range of opportunities available to young people growing up in large families was extremely limited. This consequence of high fertility did not only affect the bitterly poor social classes, though. "Even individuals not directly threatened by poverty could be forced to choose emigration," it was stated in a contemporary report, "if they could not expect to retain the level of status of their parents. Among classes engaged in small-scale production, the process of leaving the parental home seems to be governed by traditional patterns. According to local customs, and based upon the majority or minority principle, only one child is permitted to remain at home."[16]

The territories that make up modern-day Austria were certainly not marked by an especially strong tendency towards emigration abroad; conversely, those areas in which emigration played the most significant role were border regions of the empire populated by numerous minorities. In this case, we may proceed from the assumption that limited political participation, unfavorable prospects for career advancement and a certain degree of social discrimination acted as push factors. Likewise, we can assume that the increasing antagonisms between nationalities as well as between social classes after the turn of the century exerted a certain background pressure in this process. Austria had become much more unstable during the period from 1900 to 1914 than it had been in the previous decades. This influenced both social as well as personal perspectives.

*Pull factors*

Considering first the internal migration within Austria-Hungary, it is immediately obvious that the main poles which exerted an attraction upon migrants were those particular region which offered opportunities to work in expanding industries and trades. Likewise, employment chances in the service sector proved to be a pull factor, particularly for female members of the labor force. In the Austrian half of the empire, Vienna, the imperial *Residenz*, administrative center and cultural capital, exerted an enormous power of attraction. Similarly, the industrial regions of Lower Austria, Styria and Upper Austria proved to have strong drawing power. In the north, Prague and the Bohemian and Moravian industrial towns were the most attractive destinations for migration; in Hungary, it was Budapest—the metropolis and industrial center. It seems to be the case that those regions which were characterized by a high degree of internal migration showed a much lower incidence of emigration abroad. Conversely, those areas with very little internal migration were the most frequent regions of origin of overseas emigrants. According to

Heinz Fassmann, the complementary relationship which existed between emigration abroad and internal migration can be precisely calculated through the use of statistical correlation methods.[17] The validity of this position, however, is subject to certain limitations: there are a great number of cases in which the rural populace migrated first to the industrial areas of Vienna and Lower Austria, failed to achieve long-term integration within the domestic labor market and only then emigrated abroad. Those factors which were applicable to the Austrian labor market were also valid overseas: a functional labor market, jobs in industry as well as employment possibilities in the service sector. The decision to emigrate abroad —multiplied millionfold—is a very real basis for the conclusion that the market for labor in the nineteenth century had become an international one. The so-called "world system" approach refers directly to this fact and interprets it in light of the consideration that migration is a manifestation of a world labor market whose development is an integral part of the process by which peripheral societies have been integrated into the capitalist world system. The Center-Periphery Model is a component of this approach. The characteristic features engendered in a particular region by this world labor market can be explained by means of an analysis of the region's position within the world system. Regarded historically, manpower resource allocation systems have brought together a wide variety of mechanisms through which labor has been integrated into the world-wide productive market.[18]

In maintaining, as we have done above, that jobs in industry and in the service sector likewise operated as pull factors in Austria-Hungary itself, it is also necessary to make reference to one very important difference. In North America, there was still strong and broad employment growth in the agricultural sector. As a result of the acquisition of frontier territories which made available enormous tracts of highly productive farmlands, there was a steady demand for unskilled agricultural laborers in North America throughout the nineteenth century. The same can be said for other industries exploiting the rich natural resources of these lands, in particular for mining. Indeed, even before the turn of the century, only a half of all farm laborers who had emigrated from Austria-Hungary were still employed in the North American agricultural sector. While, on one hand, the number of jobs in farming had already begun to contract in the United States around the end of the second half of the nineteenth century, on the other hand, the Canadian government, in cooperation with diverse private interests, had initiated a recruitment program featuring offers of free farmland and plentiful jobs in the agricultural sector.[19] In any case, on the eve of the First World War there were hundreds of thousands of emigrants from Austria-Hungary at work in agriculture in North American—and in South America as well, though the numbers there were much smaller. It was not until the 1920s that the demand for manpower in the farming sector in North America came to an abrupt end.[20]

However, the majority of emigrants from that part of Austria-Hungary which corresponds to modern-day Austria were not employed in agriculture. The proportion of "German-Austrians" who were employed in agriculture in the United States in the year 1912 for example was 8 percent, though it should be pointed out that the inclusion of emigrants from West Hungary (Burgenland) could well have had the effect of raising this figure. The majority of these "German-Austrians" were domestic servants, miners and factory workers. Ernest Spaulding points out, however, that according to American statistics very significant numbers of "German-Austrians" were employed as skilled craftsmen and highly trained industrial workers, as office workers and employees in commerce and trade, as merchants and tailors, as well as 4.5 percent as "professionals" (doctors, lawyers, architects, artists and musicians, etc).[21] Despite the fact that there existed in the North American immigration lands what was essentially a dual labor market—long-term jobs requiring higher qualifications for native-born workers, jobs demanding hard labor and low qualifications for newly-arrived immigrants (the internationalized, ethnically segregated lowest rung on the labor market ladder)—there were nevertheless ample job opportunities and well-paying positions available for immigrants possessing special skills. An example illustrating this situation is provided by the managing directors of the Imperial and Royal Tobacco Company who complained in 1909 about the emigration of "the ablest workers from the tobacco and cigar factories in Linz, Hainburg and Iglau, as well as the Vienna plants in Ottakring and Rennweg, to New York and other cities in the United States. The workers there often earn three times more than what they make in Austria."[22] Finally, it should be pointed out that a portion of the emigrants subsequently took up completely different occupations. In conjunction with an official investigation of the emigration question in 1912 by a board of inquest appointed by the Imperial Ministry of Commerce, workers referred to the fact that one of the advantages of the United States was a very flexible labor market.[23]

Thus, for emigrants from Austria-Hungary, the higher incomes and wages in North America can also be regarded as an essential pull factor.

Indeed, as a rule, higher performance and greater productivity was demanded of the workers than had been the case in Austria; incomes tended, however, to be in general 50-100 percent higher than in Austria, and sometimes the difference was well above this range.[24] A government report indicated that the wage paid for physically demanding agricultural labor in Manitoba, Canada in 1901 was 9 Crowns per day—in Austria it was approximately half as much. Furthermore, Canada had introduced programs offering free land to emigrants and the distribution of so-called homesteads (farms that were given away by the Canadian government). Female domestic servants received, along with full board and their own private room, a salary equivalent to 30-40 Crowns per month—double the usual rate for Vienna at that time.[25] According to a 1904 consular report from Montreal, field workers earned $1.00-$1.25 per day, craftsmen made $1.50-$2.50, the monthly pay for a coal miner was $50-$60. The basic cost of living for a family of four came to about $300 per year; for a single worker living alone, it was about half that amount. In 1908 in the United States, an unskilled laborer was paid $1.50-$1.60, skilled workers received $2.50-$4.00. The monthly salary of a miner was $60 (the exchange rate was from 4.80-5.10 Crowns to the dollar). A consular report dated 1908 states that the average income of an unskilled laborer in Austria was 750-1,000 Crowns per year; a worker in a similar position in the United States received the equivalent of 1,740 Crowns.[26] In addition, it can be assumed that at least a portion of the better-qualified emigrants came with the expectation of better career chances than they had in Austria, a land in which feudal considerations of class and caste still played a role in the social system, and complicated mechanisms determined who would be promoted up the career ladder and who would not.

A portion of those who emigrated overseas did not—at least initially —do so with the intention of permanently settling abroad. Thus, compared to 170,191 persons who emigrated overseas from Austria-Hungary in 1909, there were 49,413 who returned. In 1910, there were 258,737 emigrants versus 47,290 returnees. In 1908, there were 168,509 emigrants and 130,197 returnees, which proves that those who emigrated abroad were thoroughly capable of reacting quickly to changed circumstances: North America went through a short recession in 1907 and in the year thereafter a particularly large number of returning emigrants were registered.[27] On the subject of return emigration, Heinz Fassmann maintains:

Among German-speaking, Czech and Jewish emigrants, the proportion of men and women was approximately the same and the percentage of children was high. This suggests the migration of entire families and thus the intention of permanent emigration from Austria-Hungary. In contrast to this was the wave of emigration out of the eastern regions of the Monarchy. The overwhelming majority of this group were relatively young men.... This was rather a temporary form of emigration motivated by the intention of short-term financial gain.[28]

These statistical results would suggest the conclusion that emigration from the areas which now comprise Austria was rather of a permanent character. For the region of modern-day Burgenland (then western Hungary), moreover, there exists precise categorical data which permits a detailed description of the return emigration which occurred there. In this region, the percentage of those who emigrated and then returned during the period 1899 to 1913 was 22.5 percent, consisting almost exclusively of German-speaking individuals.[29] This figure is somewhat lower than the percentages of returned emigrants recorded in Galicia, Bukovina and Upper Hungary (today Slovakia) though it is nevertheless considerable. Finally as a general rule, emigration cannot be regarded as the isolated acts of single individuals but rather must be viewed in the whole context of family members who have been left behind and especially with respect to the financial situation (e.g. debts) of the entire family. This is amply illustrated by the enormous sums of transfer payments made by these emigrants. In 1913, a government minister expressed the view that emigrants overseas in the United States and Canada possessing even the most basic sense of thrift should easily be able to put aside 600-800 Crowns per year (This corresponds approximately to the yearly wage of an unskilled labourer). In any case, over the course of 18 years, the gigantic sum of 2,283,988,000 Crowns (1,220,770,000 Crowns to the Austrian half of the empire, 1,063,218,000 Crowns to the Hungarian half) was transferred to Austria-Hungary from emigrants overseas.[30]

*Intervening Factors*

At the top of this list are, of course, the emigration policies of the prospective emigrants' lands of origin as well as the conditions of acceptance imposed by the destination countries. As has already been mentioned, the freedom to emigrate was one of the basic constitutional rights in Austria. Men who wished to emigrate had only to complete the required period of military service, though this was frequently evaded.

The entire question became the subject of a public debate during the last years before the outbreak of World War I, which led to the drafting of an emigration law. Austrian measures to regulate emigration were ultimately concentrated upon supervision of the steamship companies and the advertising campaigns carried on by their emigration agents as well as the activities of private "protective associations." The restrictions which were in effect in the Hungarian half of the empire were somewhat stricter, though they likewise did not essentially hinder emigration.[31] In 1902-03 the Hungarian government planned the so called "American Action," which operated on the principle that the loss of population could be averted by allowing the immigrants to leave without any difficulties for America and then inducing them to return to Hungary with their savings.[32]

The United States passed into law an entire series of selective restrictions—such as the Chinese Exclusion Act of 1882 which totally barred immigrants from China—but these in no way impeded emigration from Austria-Hungary. Of great and immediate relevance for subjects of the Habsburg Monarchy, however, was the introduction of much more stringent entry requirements on the east coast. These regulations were enforced from 1892 at the Ellis Island Immigration Center, the tiny island in New York harbor through which millions of immigrants were funneled into the United States. It was turned into what was essentially a quarantine station in which the emigrants were medically examined and interrogated. Those who did not comply with the social and public health standards then in force were sent back.[33] Processing on Ellis Island could be avoided by booking ship's passage in first or second class, which not only offered a much more comfortable cruise in upper deck accommodations but also brought with it a form of social segregation. First and second class passengers were not checked through on Ellis Island and could disembark in New York without having to go through many unpleasant formalities. Up to 1914, U.S. policy did not seriously restrict immigration from Austria. Indeed, until the outbreak of the First World War, other nations, such as Canada, for example, were carrying on massive recruiting drives and pursuing policies which fostered immigration into these lands.[34]

Overseas emigration was further promoted by means of intensive advertising campaigns conducted by steamship companies as well as, at times, by agents representing "colonization companies" (*Ansiedlungsgesellschaften*). Since these operated on the basis of commissions, the effort was enormous and the commitment total. Information, advertising and especially pricing policies had changed. The tickets became much more affordable. In 1913 a ticket from Hamburg to Quebec could be booked for 142 Crowns, which a well paid worker in Austria could earn in one month.[35] As well, the duration and comfort of the journey were among the aspects of emigration in which there had been decisive innovation in the quarter century prior to World War I. It essentially become easier to go abroad. Modernization within the Monarchy had also contributed to this: an extensive program of railroad construction had improved access to the harbors, and improvements in the educational system made possible the more efficient spread of information and the expansion of social communication through the press.

## COMMUNITY NETWORKS AND THE PROCESS OF MIGRATION

Persistent and enduring criticism from several analytical directions has been leveled at the use of push and pull models. Most of all, a stronger integration of psychological elements into the process of theory construction seems to be necessary. Microanalyses, in-depth interviews, diaries and biographical reminiscences show very clearly that, in the real world, a pure type of push or pull factor rarely exists. What is usually encountered is a complicated mixture of motivations. Emigration is, in any case, a concrete form of action, which in most cases can only be interpreted through a multiplicity of factors. Another approach is followed by researchers such as Charles Tilly or Ewa Moravska who suggest that push and pull models overemphasize the role of individual emigrants as independent entities at the central point of the decision making process.[36] Based upon the empirical evidence, emigrants to North America over the course of the nineteenth and twentieth centuries should much more properly be regarded as members of a collective group whose behavior can best be understood within the context of social and familial community structures. According to this view, migration is a "chain" of social networks stretching from the land of origin to the receiving society. This theoretical context was also responsible for the development of the concept of a so-called "self-generating migration" which, along with the recruitment campaigns, constitutes a particularly important form of migration.[37] The presence of emigrants in a destination location brings about the creation of a social network which is continually enlarged through the subsequent arrival of relatives and acquaintances and migration thus keeps running, so to speak, "by itself." The structures which originate in this way are by no means directly and exclusively connected with the immediate financial condition and standard of living of those individuals comprising them. The foundation of immigration is the existence of a community of one's own based upon common ethnicity, religion or national origin.

Fragmentation along ethnic, religious or national lines in the destination country was a nearly universal phenomenon among emigrants during the prewar and interwar periods. Czechs in Vienna, for example, were disproportionately concentrated in certain neighborhoods,[38] as were Slovaks and Germans in Budapest, Silesians in Berlin or Poles in the Ruhr district. In the United States as well as in Canada and South America, new arrivals almost always organized themselves into communities with others who shared their ethnic background or national origin. Germans organized themselves into groups of Swabians, Hessians and Bavarians, and there existed organizations of Styrians, German Hungarians, Bohemians, and others. Galician Jews segregated themselves in New York within their own group, separate from American or Russian Jews.[39] Besides the segregation practiced by the native-born population and in addition to the need to secure cheap accommodations, it was the desire to associate with people from the same cultural background, from the same village or rural region who spoke the same local dialect, which motivated emigrants to settle together in homogenous neighborhoods. The ability to live in close geographical proximity, the formation of ghettos, facilitated communication and promoted the formation of their own organizations, offered a form of protection from the new culture and served as an intermediate stop along the way to complete integration into the hegemonic society. In this way, the risks associated with migration were considerably lessened. By means of hundreds of thousands of letters, money transfers and return voyages, either to visit or to return for good, close contacts with the "old" community were maintained. These patterns of interwoven relationships often remained intact for decades.

In the case of the most numerous group of emigrants from the territory of modern-day Austria, the German-speaking emigrants from western Hungary (Burgenland), the most concrete illustration of the great importance attached to network formation in the process of emigration is, by far, the choice of the place of initial settlement in North America. Thus, for example, according to registration records for the region surrounding the district capital of Güssing dating from 1888, Karl Krenn and Karl Reichl emigrated in that year from the community of Limbach to Allentown, Pennsylvania. The parish chronicle of Limbach, a village of only a few hundred inhabitants, subsequently records the emigration of 74 parishioners to Allentown from this village alone. Up to 1930, more than 1,000 Burgenlanders emigrated to Allentown. A similar chain of events played itself out in connection with the town of Coplay, Pennsylvania, the site of a cement mill in the 1880s. Josef Urschik emigrated to Coplay from a tiny village near Güssing in 1884 and the news of the cement mill then spread through the villages of Gerersdorf, Neustift and Inzenhof. According to the 1910 census, Inzenhof had a population of 673, of which 98 were currently residing in Coplay, Pennsylvania.[40] The use of networks also made possible emigration from this region to metropolitan centers in North America. For his doctoral dissertation in 1913, economist Ladislaus Schneider observed emigrants in the embarkation ports of northern Germany.[41] In Hamburg, for instance, he took particular notice of entire groups of women and children from the three villages of Strem, Deutsch-Bieling and Heiligenbrunn (all in the vicinity of Güssing) who were all travelling with prepaid tickets to New York. These steamship tickets had been purchased in the United States or in Canada and then mailed to the passengers in Europe. Of 202,000 sold tickets in the year 1910, approximtely 90,000 were prepaid tickets.[42]

An additional source of evidence exhibiting the function played by networks in the process of emigration is the biographical archive, documenting the lives of 4,200 adult emigrants to the United States, compiled for the province of Vorarlberg, the westernmost crown land of the Monarchy. A collection of letters documents the decisive influence of relatives and acquaintances overseas upon the decision to emigrate. This is particularly true for female emigrants in general and, above all, for sisters and wives whose emigration can quite properly be described as a type of "mail-order delivery." Besides these bonds connecting family members, however, long-term, self-generating emigration from specific localities was also promoted by so-called patrons, who had succeeded as entrepreneurs and arranged to recruit replacement manpower from their native regions. An example of this is Franz Saler, a building contractor originally from Gaschurn in Montafon, who preferred to employ his fellow countrymen from this part of Vorarlberg in the key positions of his various enterprises in St. Louis. This fact was known to those willing to emigrate from Montafon; beginning in the 1860s, dozens of emigrants left that area to begin work in St. Louis. This procedure offered advantages for both sides: on one hand, the employee had a secure job upon arrival; on the other, the employer got a well-trained worker who was, however, totally dependent on him and therefore a source of relatively cheap labor. This remained true at least until the newly-arrived immigrant had made sufficient progress learning the new language that he no longer required the protection of his countryman and could find a better paying position on his own.[43] This process, at least within the paternalistic structure of the regional society of Vorarlberg, was interpreted as "help" and not as "exploitation."

A very wide variety of forms of migration can be observed among Jewish emigrants. Hugo Hitz, born in 1890 in Vienna as the son of a haulage contractor and shipping agent, remained in New York during the course of a business trip with his father in 1906. Before the outbreak of the First World War, he had already arranged for the emigration of one brother and two additional relatives with prepaid second class tickets. This is the classic case of familially-organized self-generating migration. However, Jewish emigration also took place through the operation of organized emigration societies. Thus, in Vienna there existed the "Machikse hadath" emigration society of religious Jews along with the "Unitas," "Patria" and "Columbus" societies organized by predominantly assimilated Jews.[44] The Columbus Society, which was founded in 1910 by the Viennese businessman Jakob Feldmann, became the subject of disparaging gossip to the effect that Feldmann was using the society more as a means to further his own business interests rather than pursuing "charitable works" as was called for in the organization's by-laws.[45] In New York and in many other cities of North America, there existed a wide variety of emigration societies and so-called *Landsmanschaftn* which were organized on a strictly regional basis: the "Erste Shendiszower Galizianer Cheva," the "Tarnopol Business Men's Association" and the "Kolomeer Frends Asosieshon [sic]" are just a few examples. The "United Galician Jews in America" had branch affiliates in Boston, Philadelphia, Detroit, Chicago, New York and elsewhere.[46] As the 6-year-old boy Isidore who later became the father of Henry Miller boarded the train in an East Galician *shtetl* after the turn of the century, he was placed in the care of a network of countrymen and relatives which accompanied him on his entire train trip, during his overnight stays until his departure from a German port, throughout his three-week steamship voyage until the very moment he was picked up by his brother at the New York pier.[47] The Jews of Galicia and Bukovina in particular, had diverse and well-functioning networks at their disposal. Up to now, there has been no record of the existence prior to 1914 of a *Landsmannschaft* explicitly dedicated to Viennese Jewish emigrants.[48]

FROM IGNORANCE TO REJECTION: THE PUBLIC
DISCUSSION OF OVERSEAS MIGRATION IN AUSTRIA

Phenomena of geographical mobility did not receive very much public
recognition in the nineteenth and early twentieth centuries. The exception was overseas migration. At the turn of the century critical, at times
polemical, articles against overseas migration abounded. The chronicle of
emigration as revealed in daily newspapers and in consular reports can be
analyzed by viewing the archival material in possession of the Austrian
*Haus-, Hof- und Staatsarchiv.*[49] The most important findings to be gained
from an examination of this material is that before 1870 articles on
migration were published only occasionally. Reports became more
numerous after 1870. The tenor of the articles and reports, especially
those in the nineteenth century, is didactic, a "raised, warning finger saying: Stay at home and feed yourself honestly."[50]

Stories of failure abounded: calls for help from families in Brazil who
had been badly affected by floods; descriptions of the labor market in
Chicago against a background of hunger and unemployment; the fate of
migrants who had been turned away in Rio de Janeiro. These reports
appeared not only in the country's major daily newspapers, but in regional and local papers as well. In the 19th century, both *Die Eisenstädter
Zeitung* and the *Oberwarther Sonntags Zeitung*, newspapers in what was
then West Hungary and later Burgenland, published immigration "horror
stories" as part of their strategy of deterrence. A common journalistic
instrument in this campaign was the publication of presumably authentic
letters from emigrants abroad, often under headlines such as "Warning to
Emigrants." These letters offered a portrayal of the fate awaiting emigrants
to America, complaining bitterly about unexpected difficulties such as the
brutality of the ocean voyage, high prices, lack of work and the ruthless
behavior of Americans towards foreign emigrants, usually ending with the
expression of the desperate wish to return. The authenticity of these
"exclusives" is indeed questionable. Particularly negative articles were
invariably published without mention of the name of the subject, as in the
case of the report of the suicide of a formerly well-to-do man who returned
impoverished from his emigration abroad or, as another example, the story
of the farmer's wife who preferred to throw herself and her children from
a moving train rather than accompany her husband into emigration. Until
after the turn of the century, the journalistic profession played absolutely
no role in the development of a concrete emigration policy.[51]

In the 1890s and more clearly since the turn of the century, the reports became partly more objective. Articles frequently mention the comparatively high wages paid by industrial and mining companies in the United States. Some authors tried to calculate the economic losses which arose from costs of upbringing, training and lost working hours. The opposite position was that migration—here once again only emigration—cannot be halted and is a "natural" result of the liberalization process of the era. Rather than futile prohibitive measures, regulations should be passed which would lead to a favorable impact of migration on the country of origin. Thus the Austro-Hungarian Colonial Society (*Österreich-ungarische Kolonial-Gesellschaft*) argued:

The feudal view of emigration, which prevailed in all European countries including Austria-Hungary and which resulted in the government trying to stop the people leaving by using strict, prohibitive measures, caused enormous losses and unhappiness on both sides, the proof of which each of us emigrants could produce. In Austria-Hungary especially, this system led to further noxious acts, above all to a shameless exploitation of the emigrants through agents. The Austro-Hungarian Colonial Society concentrated their reforming activities above all on these absurd conditions which were the natural consequences of the purely prohibitive legislation. Realizing correctly that a social phenomenon like mass emigration must not or could not be suppressed by mere police action, their basic principle was: Do not promote emigration but regulate it appropriately.[52]

In the only modern demographic work to treat this topic, Heinz Fassmann describes the attitudes expressed in the public discussion of emigration as ambivalent. An analysis of the reportage, however, shows that the mainstream press displayed a tendency to dampen the expectations of would-be emigrants even after the turn of the century. This direction was pursued in thoroughly different forms, varying according to the newspaper's political orientation and ties to interest groups and lobbies. For example, in the years 1912-1913 the Christian-Socialist *Reichspost* followed a policy of scandalizing emigration in deference to military interests, and with a view toward maintaining the status quo among the steamship lines licensed to do business by the Monarchy. Actually, at this time in the Austrian half of the empire, approximately 100,000 draftees failed to appear for enlistment, most of whom had emigrated or traveled abroad to evade military service. The newspaper's campaign had enormous political consequences and also influenced public opinion in the direction of a limitation of the right of emigration.

## THE "CANADA AFFAIR"

The immediate background of the campaign in the so-called "Canada Affair" was of limited social-political significance. The Canadian Pacific Railway Company was trying to break into the strictly regulated Austrian transportation market from which the international steamship cartel ("the pool") had up to then successfully been excluding it. However, the pool refused to consent to monitoring Austrians in German ports to determine if they were liable for military service. When Canadian Pacific submitted an offer to sail to the harbor of Trieste, which was then a part of the empire and offered the imperial military authorities far better surveillance possibilities, the Austrian government grasped the opportunity and granted the Canadian line a concession. With it, the Canadian Pacific transported 14,000 passengers in 1912 and 11,000 through September 1913. Because the line was less concerned with making a profit from its steamship business than its was with attracting settlers to its vast Canadian land holdings, its fares were comparatively low. As a result, Canadian Pacific became the target of a newspaper campaign which was most probably whipped up by its competitors in the pool. Since the entrance of Canadian Pacific into the market, their losses were approaching 10,000,000 Crowns. Most inflammatory was the *Reichspost*, which, in articles bearing titles such as "The Dirty Business of Human Freight" and "The Immigrant Hyenas," made prominent reference to the predominantly Jewish origin of various emigration agents as well as the Austrian general representative of the Canadian Pacific, Samuel Altmann. They were charged with knowingly transporting men liable for military service, and on October 16, 1913 the Canadian Pacific's concession was suspended and Samuel Altmann was arrested. Of course, all of the steamship lines had transported men evading military service, but the campaign against Canadian Pacific led to a diplomatic row with Canada, which regarded the proceedings as an unfriendly act (Altmann had both British and American citizenship). In the event it emerged that, of 2,072 punishable offenses (transporting those liable for military service), a mere 5.3 percent (111 cases) could be charged against Canadian Pacific, while most had been committed by members of the pool. Altmann was ultimately freed on bail and Canadian Pacific was permitted back in business.[53] Among the few newspapers which had taken a neutral position in the affair was the Social-Democratic *Arbeiter-Zeitung*. The working class press was generally interested in objective reporting in matters of emigration. Among other things, this had much to do with their wish to avoid negative attitudes toward emigrants, and their desire not to make it even more difficult for workers to improve their lot. Otto Bauer, the social-democratic theoretician and later party chief, spoke out in favor of the Austrian worker's freedom to emigrate to North America as early as 1907.[54]

Indeed, even after the Canada Affair, the yellow press continued to speak of "hyenas" and "the patriotic duty to speak out against emigration." The *Reichspost* labeled emigration as a "moral defect" and as a "cancer in the body of the *Volk*." In Preßburg (Bratislava, Pozsony), a dissertation in economics was accepted in which emigration was characterized as an "epidemic disease of the masses."[55] In this climate of opinion, the draft of a new emigration law was introduced to put an end to the previously liberal treatment. While the parliamentary debate was in process, the tabloids were demanding more stringent policing of the trains and the borders "to apprehend those traitors to the fatherland attempting to evade their duty." Indeed, beginning with 1 March 1914 a system of control was installed which forced the train conductors and the police to control all potential emigrants, who could be draftees.[56]

From the historical perspective, these voices in the press are to be regarded as part of a patriotic offensive that ultimately served the military interests and played a direct role in the ideological preparations for war. Alexander Fischel took up this position in the foreword to his book *The Harmful Side of Emigration and How to Fight Against It*, written just before the outbreak of the war: "I have been compelled to put together the following hasty argument because of the danger, through emigration, to our army, and therefore our position of power.... May this book have the desired patriotic success."[57] Before the political situation in Europe began to grow increasingly tense in the wake of the Bosnia Crisis of 1908, there was no public discussion of an impairment of Austria's military interests as a result of emigration. Thus, even during the Canada Affair, the *Arbeiter-Zeitung* branded a journalist of the right wing newspaper *Reichspost*, whose reporting was particularly aggressive, as "a fomenter of war in the pay of the military."[58] Finally, the outbreak of World War I ended not only the offensive by the newspapers but the deliberations of the *Reichsrat* as well and, as a result of the political events, emigration came to a standstill on its own.

## ENDNOTES

1. *Tafeln zur Statistik der österreichischen Monarchie* zusammengestellt von der k. k. Direction der administrativen Statistik (Vienna, 1828-1865); "Auswanderung aus den im Reichsrathe vertretenen Königreichen und Ländern 1850 bis 1868" in *Mittheilungen aus dem Gebiete der Statistik*, vol. 17/3 (1870), 81-99.
2. I.V. Bunzl, *Die österreichische Auswanderung bis zum Jahre 1848* (Vienna, 1932).
3. Hans Sturmberger, "Die Amerika-Auswanderung aus Oberösterreich zur Zeit des Neo-Absolutismus," *Mitteilungen des Oberösterreichischen Landesarchivs 7* (1960), 5-53.
4. "Auswanderung," as in ftn. 1 above, pp. 96-99.
5. Staatsgrundgesetz of 21 December 1867, § 141 RGB Art. 4, Par. 2.
6. Hans Chmelar, "Exportgut Mensch: Höhepunkte der österreichischen Auswanderung bis 1914" in ....*nach Amerika: Burgenländische Landesausstellung 1992* (Eisenstadt, 1992), p. 77.
7. Hans Chmelar, *Höhepunkte der österreichischen Auswanderung: Die Auswanderung aus den im Reichsrat vertretenen Königreichen und Ländern in den Jahren 1905-1914* (Wien, 1974), pp. 33-34.
8. Heinz Fassmann, "Emigration, Immigration and Internal Migration," in Dirk Hoerder and Inge Blank, eds., *Roots of the Transplanted* (New York, 1994), vol. 1, 296-302.
9. Walter Dujmovits, *Die Amerika-Wanderung der Burgenländer* (Pinkafeld, 1992), pp. 201-06.
10. *Österreichisches Statistisches Jahrbuch 1914*, vol. 33 (1914), 63.
11. Anette Treibel, *Migration in modernen Gesellschaften: Soziale Folgen von Einwanderung und Gastarbeit* (Weinheim-München, 1990), pp. 29-30.
12. Michael John and Albert Lichtblau, "Vienna Around 1900: Images, Expectations, and Experiences of Labor Migrants," in Dirk Hoerder and Horst Roessler, eds., *Distant Magnets: Expectations and Realities in the Immigrant Experience, 1840-1930* (New York/London, 1993), pp. 61-67.
13. Chmelar, *Auswanderung*, p. 58.
14. Leopold Caro, "Auswanderung und Auswanderungspolitik in Österreich," *Schriften des Vereins für Sozialpolitik* 131 (1909), 34.
15. *Ibid.*
16. Zoltan Toth, "Vier Bauernmädchen in Wien: Zu den Anpassungsmodellen der Zuwanderer," in Monika Glettler, Heiko Haumann and Gottfried Schramm, eds.,

*Zentrale Städte und ihr Umland: Wechselwirkungen während der Industrialisierungsperiode in Mitteleuropa* (St. Katharinen, 1985), p. 162.

17. Fassmann, *Emigration,* pp. 296-302.

18. Saskia Sassen, *The Mobility of Labor and Capital: A Study in International Investment and Labor Flow* (New York, 1988); Immanuel Wallerstein, *Der historische Kapitalismus* (Berlin, 1984).

19. Chmelar, *Auswanderung,* pp. 31-34.

20. Vernon Briggs, *Mass Immigration and the National Interest* (New York, 1992), p. 69.

21. E. Wilder Spaulding, *The Quiet Invaders: The Story of the Austrian Impact upon America* (Vienna, 1968), pp. 68-72.

22. *Die Soziale Rundschau* (January-June, 1909), p. 56.

23. Dirk Hoerder, "Arbeitswanderung und Arbeiterbewußtsein im atlantischen Wirtschaftsraum: Forschungsansätze und hypothesen," *Archiv für Sozialgeschichte* (1988), 401-08.

24. *Protokoll der im k.k. Handelsministerium durchgeführten Vernehmung von Auskunftspersonen über die Auswanderung aus Österreich* (Vienna, 1912).

25. Richard Riedl, *Die Organisation der Auswanderung in Österreich: Bericht über die vorläufigen Ergebnisse der im k.k. Handelsministerium durchgeführten Untersuchung* (Vienna, 1913), pp. 136-40.

26. Ernö Deak, "Die Auswanderung—eine Massenbewegung," in *Das Zeitalter Kaiser Franz Josephs,* Part 2: *1880-1916—Glanz und Elend: Beiträge* (Vienna, 1987), p. 36.

27. *Ibid.,* p. 34.

28. Heinz Fassmann, "Einwanderung, Auswanderung und Binnenwanderung in Österreich-Ungarn um 1910," *Demographische Informationen* (1991), 96.

29. Dujmovits, *Amerika-Wanderung,* p. 203; Josef Bugnits, *Die Rückwanderung im Rahmen der burgenländischen Amerikawanderung* (Graz, 1988), pp. 8-16.

30. Deak, *Auswanderung,* p. 37.

31. Julianna Puskas, *From Hungary to the United States (1880-1914)* (Budapest, 1982), pp. 92-115.

32. Albert Tezla, *The Hazardous Quest: Hungarian Immigrants in the United States 1895-1920* (Budapest, 1993), pp. 479-519.

33. Fred Wasserman, ed., *Ellis Island: An Illustrated History of the Immigrant Experience* (New York/Toronto, 1991).

34. Riedl, *Organisation der Auswanderung,* pp. 19-27.

35. *Ibid.,* p. 253.

36. Charles Tilly, "Transplanted Networks," and Ewa Morawska, "The Sociology and Historiography of Immigration," both in Virginia Yans-McLaughlin, ed., *Immigration Reconsidered: History, Sociology, and Politics* (New York, 1990), pp. 79-95, 187-240.

37. Hoerder, *Arbeitswanderung*, p. 400.

38. Michael John and Albert Lichtblau, *Schmelztiegel Wien—einst und jetzt. Geschichte und Gegenwart der Zuwanderung nach Wien* (Vienna, 1990), pp. 143-66.

39. Klaus Hödl, *"Vom Shtetl an die Lower East Side": Galizische Juden in New York* (Vienna, Cologne, Weimar, 1991), pp. 97-122.

40. Dujmovits, *Amerika-Wanderung*, pp. 98-104.

41 Ladislaus Schneider, *Die ungarische Wanderung: Studie über die Ursachen und den Umfang der ungarischen Auswanderung* (Poszony, 1915), p. 58.

42. Riedl, *Organisation der Auswanderung*, p. 100.

43. Meinrad Pichler, *Auswanderer: Von Vorarlberg in die USA* (Bregenz, 1993), pp. 26-28.

44. Chmelar, *Auswanderung*, pp. 130-32.

45. *Ibid.*

46. Hödl, *Shtetl*, pp. 178-80.

47. Arthur Miller, *Timebends* (New York, 1987), pp. 14-15.

48. Michael Weisser, *Brotherhood of Memory: Jewish Landsmanshaften in the New World* (New York, 1989), pp. 152-55.

49. Charlotte Papen, "Die Rolle der Presse in der Konsularberichterstattung und ihre Verwendung zur Regelung der Auswanderung in Oesterreich-Ungarn 1860-1900," (unpublished Ph.D. dissertation, University of Vienna, 1949).

50. Fassmann, *Emigration*, p. 302.

51. Juliane Mikoletzky, "'In Amerika, wo gar viele Dinge auf dem Kopfe stehen'... Auswanderung und Amerikabild im Spiegel deutschsprachiger westungarischer Zeitungen 1860-1910," in *.... nach Amerika*, pp. 154-71.

52. Cited in Fassmann, *Emigration*, p. 303.

53. Chmelar, *Auswanderung*, pp. 144-52.

54. Otto Bauer, "Proletarische Wanderungen," in *Neue Zeit. Wochenschrift der deutschen Sozialdemokratie* 25 (1907), 494.

55. Schneider, *Die ungarische Wanderung*, p. 121.

56. Chmelar, *Auswanderung*, p. 157.

57. Alexander Fischel, *Die schädlichen Seiten der Auswanderung und deren Bekämpfung* (Vienna, 1914).

58. *Arbeiter-Zeitung*, 25 October 1913, p. 7.

IV

AUSTRIANS ABROAD
AUSTRIAN EMIGRATION AFTER 1945

*Traude Horvath and Gerda Neyer*
*Austrian Academy of Sciences*

AUSTRIA HAS NOT OFTEN thought of itself as a country of emigration, despite its long history of outward migration flows. During the past 150 years, millions of Austrians have left the country, either of their own free will—in search of a new and better life, for travel and adventure, or out of intellectual curiosity—or by coercion—as a result of religious, racial or political persecution. Over the past few years, the Austrian Academy of Sciences has undertaken a major research project which has attempted to reconstruct Austria's many-sided emigration history from the 19th century to the present day. The study, a collaborative effort of many different scholars, is divided into four major sub-sections whose chronological parameters are the same as those adopted by the Austrian Immigration to Canada research project. The first covers migration during the era of the Habsburg Monarchy; the second deals with different migration patterns during the First Austrian Republic; the third focuses on emigration and escape between 1938 and 1945; the final part concentrates on case studies of different countries and aspects of migration from Austria since 1945.[1] In this paper, after a brief introduction to the earlier period, we present a precis of our major findings for the period after 1945.

From the middle of the 19th century, with the onset of industrialization and the expansion of new systems of transport, migration became a mass phenomenon. From the last quarter of the nineteenth century to the beginning of the World War I, at least 5 million people—almost 10 percent of the total population—emigrated from the Austrian-Hungarian empire. About 30 percent of these migrants remained in Europe and 70 percent settled overseas. Between 1876 and 1910 about 3,550,000 people left the Austrian-Hungarian Monarchy to settle overseas. More than half of them—about 1,850,000 people (51.8 percent)—were from so-called "Cisleithania," that is, the "Austrian" half of the Monarchy.[2] Most of these, about 1.5 million, settled in the United States; some 151,000 went to Canada and 158,000 emigrated to Argentina, Brazil and other South-American countries.[3] Migration to other parts of Europe also increased during that period. In 1910 about 623,000 "Austrians" were living in the German Empire and 38,000 in Switzerland.

Migration flows, which were halted by the World War, began again at the end of 1918. Austria was now reduced to a small, ethnically homogeneous German-speaking state, which was extinguished by German annexation in 1938. Although, as in the pre-war decades, most people emigrated for economic reasons, the migration patterns during this "First Republic" became more diverse. The years between 1918 and 1938 were a time when Austria, together with several other European countries, was influenced by political, social and religious ideas which were in many cases an important factor motivating emigration. For example, about 4,000 Austrians went to the Soviet Union to participate as skilled workers, technicians, engineers and scientists in the first Five Year Plan from 1928 to 1932. Another 2,000 Austrians, half of them participating actively in the Zionist movement, left Austria for Palestine. In the 1930s the growing Nazi-movement attracted many Austrians, mostly males, to Germany, some of them for political training. It is estimated that about 60,000 Austrians migrated temporarily to Nazi Germany. Despite such political and ideological motivations, however, unemployment was usually the main reason for migration. Due to immigration restrictions imposed by the traditional immigration countries like the United States and Canada, the number of Austrian overseas migrants fell to about 80,000 in the inter-war period. Between 1919 and 1937 only 34,000 Austrians migrated to the United States and a mere 5,400 to Canada. About 29,000 chose Brazil, Argentina and other South-American countries as their emigration destination.

With the annexation of Austria by Nazi Germany in 1938, emigration became a matter of expulsion and escape. More than 120,000 Austrian Jews were forced to leave the annexed Austrian territory. They had almost no choice of country of refuge, but had to go to any country willing to accept them. It is estimated that by November 1941, when "emigration" from the Third Reich was officially banned by the Nazis, about

55,000 Austrian Jews had fled to other European countries, mostly to England (31,000); 28,000 had found refuge in the United States, 12,000 in Central and South American countries; a further 28,000 Austrian Jews escaped to Asian countries, especially to China (18,000) and to Palestine (9,000).

The migration history of Austria since 1945 is usually viewed as a history of immigration to Austria or of transit-migration through Austria. Yet, it was estimated that in 1992 about 6.4 percent of all Austrians were living abroad. Migration patterns since 1945 differ from those of the pre-war periods in many respects. There was a major exodus driven by traditional economic motives during the period of uncertainty after the establishment of the Second Austrian Republic up to about the mid-1950s. Due to the improved economic situation in Austria since the 1960s, however, emigration thereafter was no longer necessary to improve living standards but became more individualized; people chose their country of destination according to their own interests and not necessarily following their predecessors. In general, most post-1945 migrants no longer depended on the social network of relatives, friends and compatriots. Rather, many migration patters were shaped more by immigration legislation of prospective receiving countries.

In most countries immigration is regulated by immigration laws and regulations. Immigration was central to the development of traditional immigration societies like the United States, Canada and Australia and is a key feature of their respective national heritages. Nevertheless, these countries have never allowed immigration to get out of control but have established policies of active intervention and regulation. The initial control mechanisms set up during the first mass trans-Atlantic migrations were based on admission criteria that rested on racial principles of exclusion. The policies of allocating quotas to certain groups of migrants were central to the immigration agenda of these governments, frequently even beyond the abolition of the official racial exclusion clauses in the 1960s and 1970s. Australia, Canada and the United States, for example, have all established preferential quotas for family-based and skill-based immigration as well as for refugees. Legislation clearly lays down specific requirements which circumscribe admission.

In contrast to these countries, immigration has not been a central part of Western European nation building or identity formation. The countries of Western Europe still refuse to allow post-war immigrants to reshape their national identities. Post-war legislation concerning foreigners has emerged partly as a consequence of Europe's guest-worker policy of the 1960s. Its principal objective is to align immigration and settlement to the immigrant's qualifications and to enshrine guarantees that his or her stay is only temporary. While France, Switzerland and Germany have been more stringent in defining this "guest-worker" status in their immigration legislation, Sweden has moved more towards accepting postwar immigrants as permanent residents. Austrians migrating to other European countries before 1993 thus found themselves confronted with rather restrictive immigration laws as laid down for guest-workers from southern European countries. Since Austria's membership of the European Economic Area (1993) and of the European Union (1995), however, its citizens enjoy freedom of work, movement and settlement in all of the member states.

One of the basic questions addressed by our research topic concerns the precise number of Austrians who have emigrated since 1945, and the specific countries of destination. These questions are difficult to answer satisfactorily because, unlike before 1938, post-war Austria has not kept migration statistics. And while the countries of destination themselves partially fill this gap, the sources available are not always comparable. What is clear, however, is that a growing number of Austrians have emigrated since 1945. Estimates suggest that about half a million Austrians or former Austrians now live abroad, though there are various types and forms of migration that apply to these people.

Within Europe the most important form of migration has been labour migration to the neighbouring German-speaking countries, especially to Germany. There, the Austrian population has been rising steadily, from 47,000 persons in 1951 to 185,000 persons in 1992. Between 1964 and 1991 more than 533,000 Austrians settled in Germany while more than 402,000 Austrians left Germany in the same period; that means that about 131,000 Austrians stayed there. As well as permanent settlement, temporary migration to Germany is also quite significant. In general it can be said that Germany hosts by far the largest Austrian community abroad. In Switzerland, on the other hand, the Austrian population has declined since the1970s, mainly due to naturalization and a low net migration. Another factor is the restrictive immigration policy of the Swiss government, which favours rotation among the foreign resident population. In 1990 there were about 30,000 Austrians living permanently in Switzerland. Another significant dimension of population movement to Switzerland and to other neighbouring countries, especially

Liechtenstein, is cross-border commuting. This form of labour migration is the daily routine for more than 60,000 Austrians. They work in a foreign country but remain resident in their own. Higher salaries are the main reason for leaving Austria to seek work in other European countries. It is these personal economic considerations that have promoted emigration, especially to Germany, Switzerland and Sweden.

While migration to other European countries can generally be attributed to personal initiatives, between 1945 and 1960 the Austrian Ministry of Labour and Austrian employment offices played an important part in initiating and facilitating it. The employment offices were involved in the mediation between foreign employers and unemployed Austrian workers willing to work abroad. Leading players in this form of organized migration were Switzerland, Belgium, the Netherlands and Great Britain. More than 10,000 Austrians, most of them women, left the country in this way. British recruitment practices demonstrate that special regard was paid to the interests of the British economy. Britain's recruitment policy had specific characteristics for non-Commonwealth citizens, while Commonwealth citizens were dealt with on separate terms. The workers recruited from Austria were placed in specific jobs, especially in mental hospitals, the textile industry and domestic services. Our study shows that Austrian women living in Britain never became fully integrated into their host society, with the exception of those who married British citizens. In most cases, however, they married foreigners. Only a fifth of the women managed to obtain better jobs while the majority remained in unskilled positions in the textile industry or in private households or unemployed. The mediation activities of the Austrian employment offices with British authorities and factories continued until 1960, though the number of persons mediated to Great Britain declined steadily. In 1960 the Austrian Ministry of Labour halted these activities as a result of the acute labour shortage in Austria itself.

Similarly, in most overseas countries to which Austrians have migrated, their number has decreased since 1945 as many of them have repatriated, become citizens of their host countries or died. American census data show that the number of Austrian-born immigrants living in the United States has declined in the past forty years from 409,000 Austrians in 1950 to 88,000 in 1990. Nevertheless, American immigration statistics show that between 1941 and 1989, 136,000 people emigrated from Austria to the United States, most of them between 1951 and 1960. Since the immigration statistics list immigrants by "country of last permanent residence," many of these migrants were probably refugees from eastern European countries. The migration pattern reflects turmoils in several Eastern European countries, as migration from Austria increased following the Hungarian Revolution of 1956, the Soviet invasion of former Czechoslovakia in 1968, and the Polish Crisis of 1980-81. According to American statistics which list the population by "place of birth," about 34,000 Austrian-born people emigrated to the United States between 1957 and 1990, about 70 percent of them between 1957 and 1970.

There is a long tradition of Austrian migration to the United States. One group of Austrians with particularly strong ties to pre-war Austrian migrants are the people of Burgenland, the Austrian province bordering on Hungary. For them post-1945 migration was made possible by their relatives in the United States. The post-war migrants chose places where relatives and acquaintances lived. Some of the post-1945 migrants from Burgenland held American passports because they had been born in the United States before World War II and had been taken back to Burgenland by their parents. Thus, some Burgenländers re-entered the United States as U.S. citizens, without knowing their country of birth—or the English language for that matter. Until the early 1970s emigration from Austria to Canada showed the same pattern. Our assessment of the Canadian data from 1946 until 1992 indicates that 38,500 Austrian citizens, 42,700 Austrian born people and 73,300 people whose last residence had been Austria emigrated to Canada. A comparison between the American and the Canadian statistics thus reveals that since 1945 more Austrians have emigrated to Canada than to the United States.

The emigration of Austrians to Australia and South Africa is basically a post-1945 phenomenon. From the turn of the century until well into the 1930s only about 1,500 Austrians appeared in the Australian census figures. The immigration of Austrians to Australia started to pick up at the end of the 1930s in the wake of racial and political persecution in Austria. The numbers of migrants were still low with the 1947 census data revealing only 4,200 Austrians. After 1945 a national program was started to provide a 2 percent population growth, concentrated on Caucasians. Partly as a result of this program advertised in Austria and partly supported by the Australian government, 24,000 Austrians emigrated to Australia as permanent or long-term migrants between 1945 and 1965. In 1952 an agreement between Austria and Australia provided financial aid for further 6,000 Austrian immigrants. After 1965, as the economic situation improved in Austria, emigration to Australia fell to a trickle. Between 1970 and 1991 only some 6,000 Austrians left for Australia, mostly highly-qualified people seeking better conditions for their professional and personal development.

Since 1945 about 25,000 Austrians have emigrated to the Republic of South Africa, about 50 percent of them directly from Austria, another 50 percent from different countries. The majority of Austrians (63 percent) entered the country between 1961 and 1975. Currently, there are some 15,000 Austrians living in the Republic of South Africa. Until recently, South Africa's immigration policy was closely linked with the apartheid system. Once in the country, white people enjoyed unexpected social and economic advancement. Most of the immigrants of the fifties left Austria for economic reasons—in order to escape the desolate postwar situation and develop freely. As a rule, they entered the country as company employees. Once their contracts expired, they went into business on their own, moving from employed to self-employed status. A number of Austrians now living in South Africa got to know the country during the 1970s through their vacations there; they entered the country as tourists, came to like it and established themselves, largely in the services sector. Well integrated into the white—and then ruling—class, the Austrians had few problems assimilating. When the democratization process was announced, a few hundred Austrians left, but the most decided to stay and face the new social and political challenges.

Many Austrians also live in Latin American countries, especially in Argentina and Brazil. Both countries have a long tradition of Austrian immigration. During the days of the Habsburg Monarchy about 150,000 multi-national "Austrians" migrated to these two countries, almost as many as to Canada (152,000); a further 28,000 Austrians settled there between 1919 and 1937, in contrast to Canada's 5,400. After 1945, on the other hand, the number of people emigrating to Latin America fell considerably as a consequence of the political and economic instability there. It is estimated that there are now about 28,000 Austrians living in Argentina and Brazil. Latin American countries have been priority countries for Austrian development projects. Until the 1960s development programs in which Austrians participated were mainly financed by church organizations, and the people who left Austria to participate in these programs did so for religious reasons. With the establishment of a government development policy in the 1960s and the foundation of several voluntary non-religious organizations, the range of people joining the development programs changed. It is estimated that about 7,000

Austrians have participated in long-term projects (those lasting more than two years) in developing countries, mostly in Latin America.

In conclusion, our study suggests that between 1945 and 1993 about 400,000 Austrians emigrated to the six major countries of destination, Germany, Switzerland, the United States, Canada, Australia and the Republic of South Africa, with about 10 percent of these emigrants choosing Canada as their new country of residence. Indications are that future Austrian emigration overseas is expected to concentrate on those emigrating for educational or professional reasons. In many fields studying or working abroad for a while has become a prerequisite for job promotion within Austria. Emigration to other European countries will likely increase with Austria's membership of the European Union, which grants freedom of movement, work and settlement to citizens of its Member States. The admission of Austria to the European Union also creates a new kind of migrant—the migrant bureaucrat. The Austrian bureaucracy—not famous for its flexibility or its mobility—is confronted with new tasks since it is forced to station its representatives and informants in Brussels. The Austrian ministries will send their own representatives to Brussels and establish bureaucratic branches there. This means a new type of civil servant is needed who will be multilingual, flexible and mobile. Austrians who have been educated or who have lived abroad will thus probably have the best chances to combine the security of a bureaucratic career with international experience.

Table 1. *Austrian citizens in 13 countries*

| country | 1950 | 1960 | 1970 | 1980 | 1990 |
|---|---|---|---|---|---|
| Germany | 46,683 | 57,337 | 143,114 | 172,573 | 183,161 |
| Switzerland | 22,153 | 37,762 | 43,143 | 31,736 | 28,802 |
| Liechtenstein | 876 | 1,184 | 1,858 | 2,029 | 2,122 |
| Sweden | 1,000 | 4,000 | 4,984 | 3,346 | 2,819 |
| Great Britain | — | 8,000 | 6,000 | 7,000 | 5,870 |
| France | 3,790 | 3,740 | 3,315 | 2,904 | 3,280 |
| Italy | 3,316 | 3,566 | 4,810 | 5,500 | 8,800 |
| U.S. | — | 26,000 | 20,000 | 18,900 | 15,700 |
| Canada | — | 13,000 | 7,500 | 10,000 | 10,000 |
| Australia | — | 14,000 | 11,000 | 10,000 | 11,000 |
| Republic of South Africa | — | 1,000 | 5,000 | 10,000 | 20,000 |
| Brazil | — | 17,000 | 21,000 | 21,000 | 21,000 |
| Argentina | — | 6,000 | 5,000 | 8,000 | 10,000 |
| Total (rounded) | | 193,000 | 277,000 | 303,000 | 323,000 |

*Source:* Abderrahim Fraiji and Adelheid Fraiji-Bauer, "Auswanderungen von Österreichern und Österreicherinnen nach 1945," in our forthcoming study, entitled *Auswanderungen aus Österreich.*

## ENDNOTES

1.   Traude Horvath and Gerda Neyer, eds., *Auswanderungen aus Österreich* (Vienna, 1996), in press with the Austrian Academy of Sciences. Contributors include Heidi Armbruster, Gabriele Anderl, Alex Belschan, Gudrun Biffl, Werner Dreier, Heinz Faßmann, Abderrahim Fraiji, Adelheid Fraiji-Bauer, Reinhold Gärtner, Johanna Gehmacher, Regina Haberfellner, Traude Horvath, Angelika Jensen, Michael John, Ulrike Lunacek, Barry McLoughlin, Peter Meusburger, Gerda Neyer, Andrea Obrecht, Monika Pelz, Meinrad Pichler, Ursula Prutsch, Ulrike Pröll, Hans Schafranek, Andrea Schmidt, Eugene Sensenig, and Elisabeth Welzig.

2.   "Cisleithania," or the "Austrian" half of the Austro-Hungarian Empire, included the provinces of Upper Austria, Lower Austria, Styria, Carinthia, Carniola, Tyrol, Vorarlberg, Salzburg, Bohemia, Moravia, Silesia, Galicia and Lodomeria, Bukovina, Goricia, Gradisca, Istria, Dalmatia and Trieste. The officially recognized language groups residing in these provinces were: German-speakers (36 percent), Czechs (23

percent), Poles (16 percent), Ukrainians (known officially as "Ruthenians") (13 percent), Slovenes (5 percent), Serbo-Croats (3 percent) and Italians (3 percent). In 1910 this portion of the Monarchy also included approximately 1.3 million Jews (4.6 percent of the total population), who had legal recognition as a confession but not as a nationality. All members of confessional groups had to declare themselves for one of the official language groups. Most Jews of Cisleithania declared themselves German or Polish. For details on the ethnic and confessional complexities of the Austro-Hungarian Empire see Adam Wandruszka and Peter Urbanitsch, eds., *Die Habsburgermonarchie*, vol. 3: *The Völker des Reichs* (Vienna, 1980), and vol. 4: *Die Konfessionen* (Vienna, 1985).

3.  For a detailed analysis of this migration see Michael John, "Push and Pull Factors for Overseas Migrants from Austria-Hungary in the 19th and 20th Centuries," above, pp. 55-81.

V

# THE LARGEST AUSTRIAN DIALECT SPEECH-ISLAND IN NORTH AMERICA

*Herfried Scheer*
*Concordia University*

THE DIALECT OF THE "HUTTERITES" or, officially, of the "Members of the Church of the Hutterian Brethren" has evolved in the diaspora, ever since their forefathers left their Austrian homelands more than 470 years ago, and they have retained the language of their ancestors throughout these centuries. Since they have always preferred to live in isolation, far away from the temptations of "The Evil World," their society has never been investigated by any scholar, until A.J.F. Zieglschmid, a professor at Northwestern University in Illinois, began to study them and published, with their cooperation, *Die älteste Chronik der Hutterischen Brüder* in 1943.[1] The first attempt at a linguistic investigation of the Hutterian dialect was made by Father Jerome J. Holtzman, who compiled a brief list of some of their dialect words in his 1960 M.A. thesis.[2] The first thorough investigation of the lexicon of the Hutterian dialect was done by this author during a decade of field work in preparation for a Ph.D. dissertation[3] and, subsequently, for his 1987 dictionary *Die deutsche Mundart der Hutterischen Brüder in Nordamerika*.[4] During the last three decades, many articles and several books have been published, some of them by sociologists and linguists from Germany and from Austria,[5] quite a few more by American historians,[6] and one book even by a (rather sensational) journalist.[7]

In order to comprehend the Hutterian way of life, one has to forget much the twentieth century has offered us—though the number of technological advances that have been embraced by the Hutterites may come as a surprise. In fact, their machinery, their tractors and combines, their plows and their hatcheries are much more up-to-date, and their milk, honey and other produce much fresher than anything that the average farmer of the Western prairies, both in Canada and in the United States, would have available. Rather, what distinguishes the Hutterites is their culture and way of life. That life is based entirely upon the Holy Scriptures. They do not merely preach the Gospel, they also live accordingly; all members of a colony (*"Bruderhof"*) attend a daily prayer at the Community Hall (they have no church as such); they sing their traditional hymns, many of them composed by, or about their martyrs, burnt at the stake as heretics during the sixteenth and seventeenth centuries; and they strictly observe paternalistic traditions. Thus, when a couple is walking, the woman will follow obediently behind the man; and when the time comes to elect a new preacher, it is only the menfolk who will cast their ballots. The Hutterites have also always had a much closer relationship with their forefathers than has been the case for any "average" European or North American.

Hutterites take their name from Jakob Hutter, a hatmaker originally from South Tyrol. He was one of the early, most energetic leaders of an "anti-ultramontane, anti-Roman-Catholic, Protestant" group who settled, or rather, had to settle, with his followers in Moravia, out of the immediate reach of ecclesiastical and secular authorities who had outlawed their sect. Hutter's followers belonged to the radical millenarian extreme of the Protestant Reformation, called "Anabaptists" by their enemies for their adherence to the principle of adult baptism. Convinced that membership in the community could come only through the voluntary commitment of the mature adult, every Hutterite man of approximately 25 years of age, and every woman of about 20 has to ask to be baptized explicitly, which means, to be admitted as a member of the Church. Hutter's followers also believed in *"Gelassenheit,"* a concept which can only vaguely be translated with "true-self surrender, a peaceful submission to God and to the believing community, together with the forsaking of private property."[8] They would never bear arms or defend themselves against their attackers, they were ardent conscientious objectors, and they consider it as much of a sacrilege to take an oath as it would be to swear. Above all, they believed in the "community of goods," as it had been practiced by the early Christians, which meant an absolute disavowal of personal property. Even to this day, all the members of the "Hutterian Church" still follow this principle strictly. Hutterites never carry money in their pockets. If someone from the community has to go to town, as does happen on rare occasions, they will go in a group and hardly ever alone. The permission to do so, as well as the amount of money that has to be paid for any approved purchase, is only granted by the preacher. All these tenets have been upheld and followed, albeit with varying consistency, throughout the centuries.[9]

After Jacob Hutter was publicly burned at Innsbruck in 1536, disunity prevailed within the community in Moravia, and rivalries arose with other Baptist sects. During the 1550s, other strong leaders were then able to reunite the Hutterites into a cohesive community of believers. The second half of the sixteenth century was the golden period in Moravia. The highly conscientious chroniclers tell us that during those five decades, there were up to 65 communities of Hutterian Brethren, with up to 20,000 and even 30,000 souls. At that time, the Hutterites were not primarily engaged in farming, as has been the predominant livelihood almost throughout their history. Many of them were artisans, some were teachers who also taught the sons and daughters of aristocrats, others were physicians who were even called to treat and heal some of the nobles in Vienna. There was also a great, renewed activity for Hutterite missionaries who travelled to outlying parts of the German lands preaching the Gospel.

With the implementation of the Counter-Reformation in Moravia at the beginning of the seventeenth century, the Hutterites began to flee eastward. Several communities moved to northern Hungary (in what is present-day Slovakia) and others to Transylvania, where they founded new settlements. These settlements, however, soon found themselves on the front lines of the Austro-Turkish conflict of that century, with the result that whole armies ransacked the meager possessions of the Hutterites, and many were killed. Deprivation and despair, enforced conversions by the Jesuits, a general loss of their morale and of their belief greatly reduced their numbers. The few surviving Hutterites from Moravia and northern Hungary joined their Brethren in Transylvania. But even there, the atmosphere was far from hospitable. By 1750 the number of originally Tyrolean Hutterites was reduced to approximately 30 or 40 individuals.[10]

The mid-eighteenth century also saw the last wave of Counter-Reformation zeal engulf the Austrian heartland. Various secret or "crypto-Protestant" sects were discovered by preachers in remote mountain valleys, and a final effort to enforce confessional uniformity set in. Most of these crypto-Protestants were sentenced to "internal exile" (or "transmigration" as it was called) to distant parts of the Habsburg Monarchy where confessional pluralism was constitutionally permitted. Among these was a group of 58 Carinthian Lutherans who were deported to Transylvania in 1755. One year later these new arrivals encountered the "30 or 40" persecuted, desperate Tyrolean Hutterites. The Carinthian newcomers were filled with enthusiasm and inspired by the still powerful religious convictions of these Tyrolean Hutterites, and the two communities amalgamated. The Carinthians accepted the principle of Community of Goods, one of the corner-stones of the Hutterian way of life, and the other Baptist tenets.

Most of Hutter's early followers came from the Tyrol, some of them from other Austrian or Upper-German speaking regions, only very few from Central Germany. Thus, the dialect of the young community in its Moravian heyday was predominantly Tyrolean. Most elements of this dialect were retained well into the eighteenth century. With this amalgamation with the slightly greater number of Carinthians, who seemed in any case to be more rigorous and more zealous in the pursuit of this newly found religion, the Carinthian dialect became predominant over the Tryrolean—a predominance which was later confirmed through lexical and phonological research.[11] The new Carinthian-Tyrolian dialectical amalgamation then survived all subsequent migratory experiences and remains the basis of the Hutterite German spoken today.

The ongoing migratory saga of the Hutterites continued in the later eighteenth century. Still harried in Transylvania by Catholic and mainstream Protestant pressures, the united community of "approximately 67 souls"[12] moved on to Wallachia. Only three years later, in 1779, it was lured to Ukraine by Russian authorities seeking settlers, and promising not only financial enducements in their farming enterprises but, above all, freedom of religion and dispensation from military service. For the next 70 years this community remained in the northern part of Ukraine where it prospered initially, but later quarrelled amongst themselves and ran into financial difficulties. Around 1840 they asked German Mennonites, who lived in the southern Ukraine, for support, and with their help they could then settle quite close to the Mennonite colonies. But again, serious problems arose when several Hutterite families decided to live on their own,[13] rather than in the traditional Community of Goods. In the early 1870s the Russian authorities threatened to revoke all the privileges they had guaranteed before. As a result all the Hutterites and many other German settlers emigrated and arrived, mostly between 1874 and 1877, in North America.

The Hutterian Brethren, who had decided to continue living on their communal farms, settled in southern South Dakota on three *"Bruderhöfe"* of approximately 50 to 80 souls each: on one such *Bruderhof* the preacher was a blacksmith, so his group came to be called the *"Schmiedeleut"*; on the next *Bruderhof* the preacher's first name was Darius, so these people were called the *"Dariusleut"*; and the third Bruderhof had a teacher as their preacher, and these became the *"Lehrerleut."* Out of this original group of three, approximately thirty *Bruderhöfe* were gradually established in the period from the 1870s until the First World War. One after another "mother" *Bruderhof* subdivided, and "daughter" *Bruderhöfe* were founded. This subdividing or "branching" occurs, as a general practice, when the number of individuals on a *Bruderhof* increases to more than 120. The separation of families and of individuals follows strict rules. Most important, a new preacher has to be elected by all the baptized men of the *Bruderhof.* A decision is then reached by lot (*"Gottesurteil"*) which group will have to move into the new quarters, and which group may stay.

During those early days in North America, the kinship bonds between the three *"Leut"* groups were still more or less intact. This was easy to achieve, since all thirty *Bruderhöfe* faced similar problems in the new land and, in particular, all of them had remained in South Dakota until around 1914. Their success, however, aroused the envy and enmity among the local population in South Dakota. Furthermore, the strange foreign ways of the Hutterites, their black garb, their isolation from society and, above all, their German language and German background made them, in the eyes of quite a few locals, "enemies of the state." Some of their property was ransacked, cattle were stolen, and two young Hutterities who had been drafted and forced to wear a uniform, were even killed by some soldiers. With the exception of the *"Bonhomme Bruderhof,"*[14] the oldest, "mother" *Bruderhof* of all *Schmiedeleut* settlements, all the other communities moved to Canada by the end of the War. Many *Bruderhöfe*—above all, the *Schmiedleut*—resettled in the United States shortly thereafter, but most *Dariusleut* and *Lehrerleut* moved on to, or rather stayed, in Alberta and Saskatchewan. Other *Schmiedeleut* preferred to settle in Manitoba. These great geographic distances between the communities which now existed, however, led to a much more pronounced separation between the three *"Leut"* groups, and during the last 120 years this split within the Hutterian community has only intensified.

Nowadays, *Schmiedeleut* work crews or a group of Sunday afternoon visitors might very well drive to another *Schmiedeleut Bruderhof.* But it is extremely rare that any member of the *Schmiedeleut* (with the exception of the preachers) would come into contact with members of another group.

Therefore, intermarriage hardly ever occurs, and since those few members of the first three *Bruderhöfe* are the forefathers of almost all the Hutterian Brethren of today, the genetic consequences can be unfortunate. The Hutterites have always been aware of these dangers. They prohibit marriages between first cousins, and they also try to forestall marriages between second cousins. That they have propered in North America can be measured by the population figures. The last official census within the group in 1974 counted 21,521 Hutterite Brethren, and present numbers may be as high as 33,000.[15]

One author has described the Hutterites as "an ethnic group, a culture, an economy, a sect ... a kind of 'nation'... peasants ... entrepreneurs ... in short, a unique people."[16] Part of what has made them so has been their centuries-long retention of their original Austrian speech pattern, yet prospects for German-language retention in North America are uncertain. To date this has been tied inextricably to the Hutterite education system. Until age three, Hutterite children spend their time in the house of the parents. From age three to six, the "little boys and girls" (*mandlen un dindlen*) attend the "little school" (*klaana schu-el*) where they learn to obey, to pray and to get along with one another. Up to that age they have hardly heard any English, except perhaps for words like "teacher, candy, first call" (instead of German "*Lehrer, Bonbon, erstes Glockenzeichen*") and other words that have begun to be used right in the middle of German sentences. Next in order of importance is the "German or big school," (*daitscha uder gruusa schu-el)* from age six to fifteen, which is attended concurrently with English school. The children meet early in the morning before "English school," they stay on every afternoon after the latter closes, and they have another German session on Saturdays. The teacher is one of the more experienced Hutterite men who teaches them to read and write the old German "Gothic script (*Fraktur*)." They sing old hymns, hear about episodes in the history of their forefathers, and are told Bible stories, all in German. The attitude of *"Gelassenheit"* is ingrained in their minds. If they misbehave, they learn to accept punishment without complaint, they learn to suppress their individuality in favour of their peer group, and they learn to submit to the authority of their elders without questioning.

Though the English school does not extend beyond the Elementary level, two trends have emerged. During the First World War the authorities in South Dakota, then in Canada, made instruction in English by state-licensed teachers obligatory. Initially many Hutterites objected strongly to their children being taught by an outsider about the "evil ways of the world." Nowadays, however, most Hutterites have not only resigned themselves to this "intrusion," they have come to recognize the importance both of knowing English and of understanding something about mathematics and science, and about the not-always-evil culture of the people around them. In addition, until about twenty years ago, it was only outsiders, non-Hutterites, who were allowed to teach in these English schools, because they were the only ones who had the required formal training. Since then, several young Hutterites have obtained the required teaching certificates, and now teach English to young Hutterites.

Both trends represent the daily onslaught of the American-English world that surrounds the Hutterites. Though they still use their peculiar German dialect in their every-day conversations, there are indications that English has infiltrated their religious life. To begin with, the *Älteste Chronik der Hutterischen Bruder* has recently been translated into English. Since the language of the original cannot be understood without at least some knowledge of Early New High German, this translation was absolutely necessary to make certain that every preacher has access to the contents of this old document. Secondly, it is occasionally reported that some Hutterites' Sunday services, in particular the sermon, are delivered in English. Finally, the close bonds between the *Schmiedeleut* and the most recent members of the "Church of the Hutterian Brethren" who settled on *Bruderhöfe* in the eastern United States, in Britain and Germany, even in Japan, led to a continuous exchange of letters and visitors, which are most easily carried on in English.

During the first 340 years in their history, from the 1530s until the 1870s, the Hutterites were exposed to Czech, Slovakian, Rumanian, Russian, Ukrainian and Mennonite influences upon their original Tyrolean-Carinthian dialect. Few elements in their present-day speech, however, show Slavic or Rumanian influences. No more than about forty words are distinctly Russian or Ukrainian. Besides such Russian-Ukrainian words as *tschainik* (tea kettle, or *Teekessel* in German), which might also be understood by a few speakers of Austrian dialects today, the Hutterites have one especially intriguing Slavic word in their everyday language: *svat*, and the semi-German hybrid parallel *svatin*. Neither German nor English have an equivalent. Rather, these terms are indicative of the close family ties, which are both typically Slavic and Hutterian: the relationship between the father of the son and the father of the daughter-in-law and, respectively, the relationship between the mother of the daughter and the mother of the son-in-law.

In the last 125 years, on the other hand, the overpowering influence of American English upon the everyday speech of the Hutterites of today has increased to approximately 10 percent in their lexicon, even in their pronunciation. While the influence of American English on the lexicon of the Hutterian dialect has been extensively documented[17] the influence on the Hutterites' syntax has not yet been investigated. When they say, for example, *"weil er mi nit hat gegleicht"* ("because he didn't like me," or, in modern German, *"weil ich ihm nicht gefallen habe"*), we may think we detect an anglicism in the use of the verb "to like." Yet, *"gleichen"* to mean "to like" was even used in Early New High German, and that this very verb occurs in the *Älteste Chronik*, in an entry from the year 1586: *"Weil Inen die Sach nit gleichen wolt,"* that is, "because they didn't like that."[18] On the other hand, while the word order in the sentence *"weil er mi nit hat gegleicht"* has no doubt been influenced by their dialect, a surprising feature in the pronunciation, within this phrase and a good many other dialect words, is the use of the retroflex "l" and "r," a feature that can only have been a carry-over from American English.

For the present, however, German language usage remains strong, and the peculiar Tyrolian-Carinthian dialect survives. Given that the first three *Bruderhöfe* have branched from North Dakota into a vast network of communities from Manitoba, Saskatchewan, Alberta, to British Columbia in Canada, and from North Dakota, Minnesota, Montana to Washington State in the United States, it could well be argued that the Hutterites represent the "largest" Austrian dialect speech-island in North America.[19]

## ENDNOTES

1.  A.J.F. Zieglschmid, ed., *Die älteste Chronik der Hutterischen Brüder: Ein Sprachdenkmal aus frühneuhochdeutscher Zeit*, commonly called the *Gross-Geschichtsbuch* (Ithaca NY, 1943). Zieglschmid also published *Das Klein-Geschichtsbuch der Hutterischen Brüder* (Philadelphia, 1947).

2.  Jerome J. Holtzman, "An Inquiry into the Hutterian German Dialect," (unpublished M.A. thesis, University of South Dakota, 1960). Several decades before Holtzman's investigation, some research had been done by scholars in other fields. Cf. Rudolf Wolkan, *Die Hutterer: Österreichische Wiedertäufer und Kommunisten in Amerika* (Vienna, 1918); idem, ed., *Geschichtsbuch der Hutterischen Brüder* (Vienna and Stand-Off Colony, Macleod, Alberta, Canada, 1923); Frantisek Hruby, "Die Wiedertäufer in Mähren," *Archiv für Reformationsgeschichte* 30 (1933), 1-36,

170-211; 31 (1934), 61-102; and 32 (1935), 1-40. More fundamental research was done in later years by Robert Freidmann in *Hutterite Studies* (Goshen IN, 1961); and in "A Hutterite Census for 1969: Hutterite Growth in One Century, 1874-1969," *The Mennonite Quarterly Review* 44 (1970), 100-05.

3. Herfried Scheer, "Studien zum Wortschatz der Mundart der Hutterischen Brüder. A Lexicological Analysis of the Hutterian German Dialect," (unpublished Ph.D thesis, McGill University, 1972), based in part on my earlier investigation "Sprachliche Untersuchung der ältesten Chronik der Hutterischen Brüder," (unpublished M.A. thesis, University of Alberta, 1962).

4. Herfried Scheer, *Die deutsche Mundart der Hutterischen Brüder in Nordamerika* (Vienna, 1987). Cf. also my "Research on the Hutterian German Dialect," *Canadian Ethnic Studies* 1 (1969), 13-20, and "Die älteste deutsche Sprachinsel in Nordamerika," *Germanistische Mitteilungen des Belgischen Germanisten- und Deutschlehrerverbandes* 4 (1976), 101-04.

5. Maria Hornung, "Mundart und Geschichte," in Österreichische Akademie der Wissenschaften, ed., *Studien zur österreichischbairischen Dialektkunde* (Vienna, 1967); Kurt Rein, *Religiöse Minderheiten als Sprachgemeinschaftsmodelle: Deutsche Sprachinsel täuferischen Ursprungs in den U.S.A.* (Wiesbaden, 1977).

6. Victor Peters, *All Things Common: The Hutterian Way of Life* (Minneapolis, 1965); John A. Hostetler, *Hutterite Society* (Baltimore, 1974).

7. Michael Holzach, *Das vergessene Volk: Ein Jahr bei den deutschen Hutterern in Kanada* (Hamburg, 1980).

8. Hostetler, *Hutterite Society*, p. 31.

9. G.H. Williams, *The Radical Reformation* (London, 1962); C.P. Classen, *Anabaptism, A Social History* (Ithaca NY, 1972).

10. This number can be estimated on the basis of an entry in *Das Klein-Geschichtsbuch*, p. 299, where the chronicler tells us that the united Tyrolean-Carinthian community numbered "ungefähr bei 67 Seelen" in 1767.

11. Scheer, as in footnote 4.

12. *Das Klein-Geschichtsbuch der Hutterischen Brüder*, p. 299.

13. These *"Abgefallene,"* (renegades), also came to North America, together with the Hutterian Brethren, and originally settled in South Dakota as well. They continued living on their own and came to be called the *"Prairieleut."*

14. The preacher of the Bonhomme Bruderhof treasures the hand-written original of the *Älteste Chronik der Hutterischen Brüder*. I was granted the honour of reading parts of this document from the 16th to 18th centuries.

15. Hostetler, *Hutterite Society*, p. 295. The estimate given above, of about 33,000 Brethren, is based on later conversations with various Hutterites. This number does not include, however, those several hundreds of the most recent (English-speaking

and German-speaking!) members of the "Church of the Hutterian Brethren" who founded their "colonies" in the eastern United States, in England and Germany, and even in Japan.

16. John W. Bennett, *Hutterian Brethren* (Stanford CA, 1967).
17. Scheer, *Die deutsche Mundart der Hutterischen Brüder.*
18. *Älteste Chronik*, p. 546
19. Scheer, "Die älteste deutsche Sprachinsel."

# VI

# THE TRUDEAU-KREISKY CONNECTION
## AUSTRIA AND CANADA ON THE ROAD TO CANCÚN

*Oliver Rathkolb*
*Bruno Kreisky Forum for International Dialogue*

WHEN INQUIRING ABOUT COMMON denominators in post-1945 Austrian-Canadian relations, one seldom thinks of direct bilateral linkages, but of the common reality of an extremely strong neighbour: in the case of Austria it is Germany, and in the Canadian case the United States of America. What Canada and Austria have in common, as Harald von Riekhoff and Hanspeter Neuhold have proposed in a recent publication, is that they are both "Unequal Partners" in the relationship with their respective neighbours.[1] In the 1970s, however, another common denominator could be adduced. Both Austria and Canada were dominated by charismatic prime ministers with high international profiles: Bruno Kreisky and Pierre Elliott Trudeau. Both men were interested in global issues and tried to take part in global debates. Though neither had either the economic or military clout of a major power, the influence of both considerably exceeded the real might of the states they represented. These common interests led to the gradual development of a very interesting bilateral relationship culminating in the first so-called "North-South Summit," the International Meeting on Co-operation and Development held on Cancún Island, Mexico, in 1981.[2]

In the 1970s diplomatic relations between Austria and Canada were characterized, on the whole, by polite friendship without any major incidents. The Canadian Foreign Minister, Allan MacEachen, visited Austria in 1976,[3] and thereafter the dialogue and flow of information on the diplomatic level increased gradually. During that time Austria was able to report a modest positive balance of trade with Canada, amounting to 301 million Austrian Schillings (c. $20 million) in 1975, 178 million in 1977 (c. $12 million), 444 million in 1978 (c. $30 million), and 174 million in 1979 (c. $11.5 million).[4] In 1980 there was a turn-about as a result of protectionist measures against Austrian exports to Canada and an increase in Canadian imports to Austria. At a time of economic difficulties in both Canada and Austria, bilateral relations were dominated by the economic agenda of each. Such homely questions as the "Emmenthaler Cheese" issue (which was to be produced in Canada after 1978, thereby resulting in customs negotiations) were probably the prickliest bones of contention between the two countries.[5]

The most important political issues discussed on the diplomatic level between these two countries were more or less "sideshows" of the every-day bilateral scheme. They focussed on the problem of east European refugees, the international disarmament negotiations and the Middle East conflict. In all these issues the national interests of both countries seemed to complement one another. From 1976 the number of people from East-ern Central Europe requesting asylum in Austria was steadily rising— from 1,818 in 1977 to 8,646 in 1980.[6] The Austrians were interested in transferring as many of these refugees to other destinations, since Austria conceived herself as a transit station, not as a classic "immigration coun-try."[7] During the Polish crisis of 1981 the Austrian government feared that public opinion might change and turn against the refugees. The influx of refugees from Poland continued unabated, and while the major-ity of the Austrian people were prepared to grant political asylum, they were reluctant to grant permanent residence status. From the point of view of politicians and diplomats in Vienna, Canada still was considered the kind of country able and willing to absorb larger numbers of immi-grants.[8] Therefore Austrian officials tried to convince the Canadian gov-ernment to increase the immigration quotas for this group of refugees and to accept a new wave of Eastern European migrants into Canada. In August 1981, after the establishment of military dictatorship in Poland, the total number of refugees in Austria for whom food and housing was provided increased to 13,873 (72 percent of whom were from Poland). As a result of a personal appeal by Kreisky to Trudeau, Canada agreed to expand its quota and resettle 3,000 Eastern European refugees from Aus-tria—three times the original number planned.[9]

Both Austria and Canada were also very much interested in the dis-armament negotiations—Canada especially pressing for a continuation of the SALT process and an overall stop of production of nuclear material for military weapons (being an important exporter of atomic power plant technology). Within the Conference on Security and Co-operation in Europe Canada in general sided with NATO policy. Initially adopting a reserved position on the issue of an European disarmament conference, Canada demanded a clear definition of the "confidence building measures" and an expert meeting on the human rights question.[10] Austria, which was more eager to see the process move forward, introduced concrete proposals concerning confidence building measures together with other neutral and non-aligned countries.[11] As a consequence, Canada began to support the non-bloc countries interest in securing the continuity of the conference by institutionalizing the all-European security efforts through a permanent organ.[12]

In the Middle East Conflict, Canada did criticize the official Israeli policy on Jerusalem and West Bank settlements, but on the whole tended tended to be largely sympathetic towards the Israeli position.[13] From the mid-1970s Austria's position tended to be more pro-Palestinian. Kreisky, in particular, tried to convince European and American politicians to accept the Palestinian Liberation Organization, represented by Yasir Arafat, as an equal negotiating partner in the various peace talks.[14] Though there was no indication that Canada was prepared to oppose the United States on such a vital issue as Jimmy Carter's Camp David policy, which excluded direct involvement by the PLO, a countervailing trend of positive relations with Arab countries nevertheless began to set in when Trudeau became the first Canadian prime minister to visit Egypt in November 1980. Subsequent visits to North Yemen and Saudi Arabia were mainly intended to get Saudi Arabia to participate in the North-South-Summit, but also brought concrete economic results for Canada. The Saudi Oil Minister, Sheikh Jamani, announced an increase of the oil exports to Canada by 100,000 barrels per day (in 1979, 40 percent of the Canadian oil imports came from Saudi Arabia). Trudeau used the opportunity to ask Canadian businessmen not to concentrate so predominantly on the U.S. market, but also to try to find markets overseas, including in Arab countries.[15] Both countries, in short, pursued policies of relatively marginal honest brokers, seeking a diplomatic middle course in the Near East.

But perhaps the most high profile aspect of Austro-Canadian bilateral relations in this period was the two countries' impact on the first North-South Summit. Here, Austria and Canada began on a different footing in this issue. While Canada already had a sound political tradition in this international issue and solid basis in academic research and non-governmental organization activities,[16] Austria's reputation was largely due to one man: Bruno Kreisky.[17] While serving as Foreign Minister of Austria from 1959 to 1966, he invested a lot of energy in keeping the political and intellectual debate on international development and co-operation going, and was influential in the establishment of the Vienna Institute for Development and Co-operation. Very much influenced by anti-colonial trends in the Socialist movement in the inter-war period, Kreisky was a pragmatic politician searching for a global niche for Austrian foreign policy to supplement the traditional interest in reducing Cold War tensions and advocating détente and disarmament.[18]

During 1975-1980 the North-South-Conflict began to be discussed on various levels: at the Conference for International Cooperation in Paris; at the United Nations, resulting in Resolution 34/138; at the fifth United Nations Conference on Trade and Development conference in Manila; and at the third United Nations Industrial Development Organization conference in New Delhi.[19] Since all these negotiations did not result in concrete solutions, the President of the World Bank, Robert McNamara, proposed setting up a committee of highly respected individuals from the global community to work on the issue. His idea led to the so called Brandt Commission, headed by the former West German Chancellor, and then Chairman of the Socialist International, Willy Brandt.[20] In his report Brandt suggested a North-South Summit on the highest level to break the negotiation logjam of the international organizations.[21] Although Kreisky was rather skeptical about any positive outcome of such a summit during his meetings with Brandt in February 1980,[22] Brandt was able to gain international support after his official presentation of the proposal at the United Nations, and at subsequent talks in the United States, Canada and Mexico.[23] The President of Mexico, Lopez Portillo, was prepared to host the conference on the resort island of Cancún, provided that a head of state from an industrialized country joined in the effort.[24]

At this point Kreisky again was asked to participate—this time by the Secretary General of the United Nations, Kurt Waldheim—and to assume the co-chairmanship with Lopez Portillo.[25] During a meeting in Salzburg on April 22, 1980, Brandt, Kreisky and the Mexican Foreign Minister, Castaneda, decided upon the countries which would constitute the nucleus group. These were to be Algeria, France, India, Saudi Arabia, Yugoslavia and Canada.[26] As Canada's interest in North-South issues had been of long standing, and her international reputation was highly respected, Portillo personally invited Prime Minister Trudeau to partici- pate in further planing.[27] Trudeau quickly began a lobbying campaign for such a summit during the G-7 meeting in Venice (June 1980) and was able to get a positive responses from both U.S. President Jimmy Carter and German Chancellor Helmut Schmidt.[28] After Carter's electoral defeat, the attitude of the Americans—now represented by the Reagan administration—cooled considerably. Trudeau intensified his efforts to convince the United States to participate in the summit during the sub- sequent G-7 meeting in Ottawa. For a while it even appeared that he had succeeded. A Canadian announcement that the United States had moved towards participation, however, was quickly denied by the American administration's official spokesmen. The American position was, in fact, more succinctly articulated by the *Wall Street Journal* when it editorial- ized, on August 5, 1980: "the global negotiations clearly are a bad idea, or more precisely, an atrocious idea."[29]

Although Trudeau thus did not succeeded in transforming the G-7 meeting into a preparatory meeting for the Cancún summit, he never- theless continued his efforts. During two state visit tours—one in November 1980 (Saudi Arabia, North Yemen, Egypt , West Germany and France) and one in January 1981 (Austria, Algeria, Nigeria, Senegal, Brazil and Mexico)—he tried to win active support for the summit. He thus managed to convince Saudi Arabia to participate despite her fears that criticism of her financial contributions and the role of OPEC would be discussed.[30] Trudeau's enthusiasm went so far that he was even prepared to discus a follow-up strategy to the summit, and in his discussions with Helmut Schmidt, he proposed an institutionalization of this North- South-Dialogue (perhaps even with long-range personal ambitions in the background).[31]

Trudeau and Kreisky planned to work on the details of the summit preparations in person, as there was some disagreement over the role the Soviet Union might play.[32] Preceding his meeting with Kreisky with a ski vacation, however, Trudeau found himself sealed off in Lech am Arlberg by a snowstorm. The planned meeting with Kreisky in Salzburg never came off. Discussions were restricted to telephone conversations, and Kreisky took over the scheduled meeting with the waiting Canadian press corps.[33] Little could anyone have known then that Trudeau would soon take over Kreisky's co-chairmanship. Due to serious health problems the Austrian Chancellor, in the event, could not fly to Cancún. Ten days before the summit Kreisky tried to convince Trudeau to take over his position. In a telephone conference Trudeau refused at first, but agreed if accepted by all participants. As Lopez Portillo insisted he was not prepared to act alone, Trudeau was more or less forced into co-chairmanship. He accepted just one night before the summit.[34]

The Cancún summit took place on 22-23 October 1981. Twenty-two heads of state and government attended and some 3,000 journalist covered the event. Although the Austrian delegation was included in the discussion with the Mexican and Canadian diplomats, its capacity to influence the conference decision making in any decisive manner had evaporated. In any case, judged by the final declaration, the results of the discussions were meagre. It stated simply that

the Heads of State and Government confirmed the desirability of supporting at the United Nations, with a sense of urgency, a consensus to launch global negotiations on a basis to be mutually agreed and in circumstances offering the prospect of meaningful progress. Some countries insisted that the competence of the specialized agencies should not be affected.[35]

Trudeau had hoped to salvage more than this from the summit with the following compromise formula:

[It is] ...recommend[ed] to the Secretary-General of the United Nations, to convene, after appropriate consultations and by the end of the year, an informal group to discuss preparations for an acceptable process of global negotiations in circumstances offering the prospect of meaningful progress. The heads of government undertook to keep in close touch in the intervening period and to act through designated personal representatives.[36]

But this compromise failed and Trudeau did not hide his disappointment. He publicly criticized Austria, Algeria and Venezuela for not having accepted the Canadian draft resolution:

I guess those who rejected it most strenuously were Venezuela and Austria. They ended up with a statement that President Portillo and I made, to the effect that global negotiations must proceed in the United Nations. But they indicated no steps beyond that. We had a formulation which would have kept the United States at the table in an effort to define the conditions for the pursuit of global negotiations, and I think that is the better procedure.... But for the Austrians and Algerians it is going to the United Nations and making more speeches—and maybe this is correct. Maybe I am wrong. Maybe the

United States will listen to those speeches and say, "Ah, we are persuaded.".... But I think
it was a tactical error on the part of several countries involved in rejecting the Canadian
compromise.[37]

This was hardly the way the Austrians saw it.

Kreisky's foreign policy advisor, Georg Lennkh, who was involved
in the summit preparation from the very beginning, disagreed with
Trudeau's account. On the one hand, the Group of 77 needed time and
was not prepared to accept the Canadian formula right away, though
there was a good chance it might do so in due course. On the other hand,
the unexpected and last-minute position of the U.S. delegation, headed
by President Reagan, that under specific circumstances the "United States
would be willing to engage in a new process" of global negotiations,
showed that though the United States preferred bilateral dialogues or a
dialogue on the level of established UN institutions, it was obviously was
prepared to go further. Yet Trudeau and the Canadian delegation were not
willing or able to sound out the real fall-back position of the United States
at that time. They also did not attempt to inform the decision makers
within the Group of 77 about the possible options buried in the American opening statement.[38]

In conclusion, Canada and Austria—represented by Trudeau and
Kreisky—successfully lobbied bilaterally in favour of the first North-
South-Summit in history. It was indeed a success that such a conference
took place at all. Despite major changes in the world's economic and
political systems, and despite some setbacks for developing countries since
then, the original analysis of the Brandt Report and the Cancún summit
still appear valid today.[39] Unfortunately the mutual interests of Austria
and Canada to have Cancún succeed could not be transformed into common strategy during the summit itself. Perhaps this was due to a different
evaluation of the American position, and to undue sensitivity on the part
of the Group of 77, which might have been prepared to accept a revised
version of the Canadian formula if not be pressed too hard into a "take it
or leave it" position. President Julius Nyerere of Tanzania, for example,
later suggested that one day more would have solved all the differences.[40]
In contrast to Trudeau, who even omitted the Cancún summit from the
text of his published memoirs,[41] Chancellor Bruno Kreisky tried to carry
on the task of pleading in favour of global negotiations on development
issues after 1981.[42] He did so despite the fact that the neo-conservative
trend advocated by American President, Ronald Reagan, and British

Prime Minister, Margaret Thatcher, the debt crisis of 1981-1982, which blocked access to financial markets for many developing countries, and the growing tension in East-West-relations, hindered further efforts.

## ENDNOTES

1. Harald von Riekhoff and Hanspeter Neuhold, eds., *Unequal Partners: A Comparative Analysis of Relations Between Austria and the Federal Republic of Germany and Between Canada and the United States of America* (Boulder CO/San Francisco CA/ Oxford, 1993).

2. For literature providing an overview of development issues, including an evaluation of Cancún, see Khadija Haq, ed., *Global Development: Issues and Choices* (Washington DC, 1983); Alexander G. Friedrich, *Der Nord-Süd-Dialog zu Beginn der 80er Jahre* (Baden-Baden, 1982); G. Braun, *Nord-Süd-Konflikt und Entwicklungspolitik* (Opladen, 1985); R.A. Mortimer, *The Third World Coalition in International Politics* (New York, 1980).

3. Bruno Kreisky Archives Foundation, Vienna [henceforth cited as BKA]: Country File Canada, *Briefing Book*, Trudeau Visit, January 1981, p. 3.

4. *Ibid.*, p. 21.

5. *Ibid.*, pp. 21-24.

6. *Ibid.*, p. 46.

7. More details on this Austrian position in Gernot Heiss, Oliver Rathkolb, eds., *Asylland wider Willen: Flüchtlinge in Österreich im europäischen Kontext seit 1914* (Vienna, 1995).

8. Heinz Fassmann and Rainer Münz, *Einwanderungsland Österreich? Historische Migrationsmuster, aktuelle Trends und politische Maßnahmen* (Vienna, 1995).

9. BKA: Correspondence, Heads of State, Kreisky to Trudeau, 14 August 1981 and Trudeau to Kreisky, 22 October 1981.

10. *Ibid.*, Country File Canada, *Briefing Book*, Trudeau Visit, January 1981, p. 7.

11. Antony J. Dolman, "The Like-Minded Countries and the North-South Conflict," *Österreichische Zeitschrift für Politikwissenschaft* 10 (1981), 153.

12. Vojtech Mastny, *Helsinki, Human Rights and European Security* (Durham NC, 1986), p. 69.

13. BKA: Country File Canada, *Briefing Book*, Trudeau Visit, January 1981, p. 11.

14. For more details on Kreisky's Middle East policies see Otmar Höll, "The Foreign Policy of the Kreisky Era," *Contemporary Austrian Studies* 2 (1993), 39-42; Oliver Rathkolb, "Bruno Kreisky: Perspectives of Top Level U.S. Foreign Policy Decision Makers, 1959-1983," *ibid.*, 137-44.

15. BKA: Country File Canada, Transcript of the Prime Minister's press conference, 17 November 1980, pp. 3-4.

16. BKA: Country File Canada, *Briefing Book*, Trudeau Visit, January 1981, p. 26. Compare, for example, the political framework for NGOs in Canada in Tim Brodhead and Brent Herbert-Copley, *Bridges of Hope? Canadian Voluntary Agencies and the Third World* (Ottawa, 1988).

17. For more details on the development policiy of Austria in the 1970s and early 1980s see Otmar Höll, *Österreichische Entwicklungshilfe, 1970-1983: Kritische Analyse und internationaler Vergleich* (Vienna, 1986); Karl A. Kumpfmüller, "Austria's development policy in the 1970s: a contribution towards closing the gap?" (unpublished Ph. D. thesis, University of Bologna, 1977).

18. Höll, "Foreign Policy," pp. 42-46.

19. Lothar Brock, "Nord-Süd Beziehungen," in Andreas Boeckh, ed., *Internationale Beziehungen*, volume 6 of Dieter Hohlen, ed., *Lexikon der Politik* (Munich, 1993), pp. 333-34.

20. Charles P. Oman, *The Postwar Evolution of Development Thinking* (London 1991), p. 111.

21. Willy Brandt et al., *North-South: A Program for Survival* (The Report of the Independent Commission on International Development Issues) (Cambridge, 1980).

22. BKA: Cancún File, Georg Lennkh, *Der Weg nach Cancún*, p. 6. Lennkh also reported that in a speech before the United Nations Kreisky warned that a summit meeting could not solve the economic problems on the agenda.

23. Vienna Institute for Development and Cooperation, ed., *The World Ten Years After the "Brandt Report": A Conference Report* (Vienna, 1989), pp. 3-13.

24. BKA: Cancún File, Lennkh, p. 7.

25. Wolfgang Benedek, "Österreichs Außenpolitik in den Nord-Südbeziehungen," in Renate Kicker, Andreas Khol and Hanspeter Neuhold, eds., *Außenpolitik und Demokratie in Österreich: Strukturen—Strategien—Stellungnahmen* (Salzburg, 1983), p. 326.

26. BKA: Cancún File, Lennkh, p. 7.

27. *Ibid.*, p. 11.

28. *Ibid.*, p. 12.

29. *Ibid.*, p. 13.

30. BKA: Country File Canada, Report 10 Pol 1980, 11 December 1980, pp. 1-7.

31. *Ibid.*, p. 5.

32. *Ibid.*, Telex from the Austrian Embassy, Ottawa, 17 December 1980.

33. BKA: Correspondence, Heads of State, Trudeau to Kreisky, 15 January 1981.

34. BKA: Cancún File, Lennkh, p. 51.

35. *Ibid.*, p. 55.
36. *Ibid.*, p. 59.
37. *Ibid.*, pp. 60.
38. *Ibid.*, p. 62.
39. G.K. Helleiner, "North South Issues in the 1980s and 1990s: Reflections on the Brandt Report," in Bruno Kreisky Forum for International Dialogue (ed.), *From Cancún to Vienna: International Development in a New World* (Vienna, 1993), p. 18.
40. BKA: Cancún File, Lennkh, p. 63.
41. Pierre Elliott Trudeau, *Memoirs* (New York, 1994).
42. Bruno Kreisky, "The McDougall Memorial Lecture," delivered before the Conference of the United Nations Food and Agricultural Organization, Rome, 7 November 1983 (Published by the Vienna Institute for Development, Occasional Papers 83/3); Bruno Kreisky and Humayun Gauber, eds., *Decolonization and After: The Future of the Third World* (London, 1987). For a critical analysis of Kreisky's proposal concerning a Marshall Plan for the Third World, which he thought should be a part of any new economic order (both before and after the Cancún summit), see Dorit Kramer-Fischer, "Ein Neuer Marshall-Plan für die Dritte Welt: Der österreichische Vorschlag zu einem verstärkten Ressourcentransfer," *Österreichische Zeitschrift für Politikwissenschaft* 10 (1981), 139-52.

# VII

# THE EMPIRE REPLANTED
## THE ENRICHMENT OF CANADA'S MUSICAL LIFE BY AUSTRIAN IMMIGRANTS IN THE TWENTIETH CENTURY

*Paul McIntyre*
*University of Windsor*

IT DOESN'T HAPPEN EVERY DAY that a group of refugees brings about major and lasting change in the country where they have found a new life. To define one's place in a strange new land is usually struggle enough; any cultural change is more likely to be worked upon the newcomer than within his or her newly adopted home. A major exception to this pattern concerns a small group of highly trained musicians, born and raised either in Austria proper or in the various provinces of the former Empire where Austrian cultural values prevailed. Much that is taken for granted in Canada's musical life today can be traced to the work of these musical missionaries. Who were they, how did they get here, and what did they do after they arrived?

Before answering those questions, we might first consider how musically abundant were the lives these people had led prior to emigration. At least since the Middle Ages, music has been central to Austrian culture, and increasingly in modern times, the rest of the Western World has looked to the music of Austrian composers as a sort of ideal. The very words "Classical Music" define the musical language of Haydn and Mozart, of Beethoven and Schubert, and of the symphonic tradition which they set in motion. In a rather different way, the self-consciously Bohemian music of Dvorak and Smetana, with its not very subtle political sub-text, opened doors to the world of nationalistic music. The mutual cross-seeding of folk and art music is an important trait of all Austrian music; one hears it in the music of such very different composers as

Haydn, Brahms and Gustav Mahler. The outlines of modern music scholarship were set out in the 1880s by the Viennese musicologist Guido
Adler. And then there is the music of the Second Viennese School, of
Arnold Schoenberg and his students, Alban Berg and Anton von Webern,
music which redefines, at the beginning of our century, the very nature of
music and so has exercised a profoundly influential effect on the course of
art music worldwide.

How much of all this penetrated the snow-bound wilds of Canada?
In the years before the end of World War II, not very much. If your town
had an orchestra, you might hear one of a handful of the symphonies of
Mozart or Beethoven, but there were precious few decent orchestras. If
you had taken piano lessons as a child, you might have had a few of the
better known keyboard pieces inflicted on you at weekly encounters—
Beethoven's "Für Elise," for example, or Dvorak's "Humoresque." If you
sang, you would certainly have found Schubert, most likely in one of his
settings from Shakespeare. If you danced the waltz, as some of us still did
in those far-off days, you would have known something of the Strauss
family. But of the higher realms of Austrian musical art and the culture
that produced it, you would have found very little.

Reasons for Canadian ignorance in the matter of European musical
culture are not hard to find. Throughout the nineteenth century, immigration to English-speaking Canada was almost entirely from the British
Isles, and the English culture remained dominant in the new country even
after the arrival of large numbers of German, Italians and Slavs at the turn
of the new century. Life under the British flag had many good things to
recommend it, but an enriched musical environment was not one of
them. For nearly two hundred years after the death of Purcell in 1695, art
music in the British Isles had been pretty much an imported phenomenon, centering largely on the personalities of two German visitors, Han-
del in the eighteenth century and Mendelssohn in the nineteenth. With
the single exception of one famous oratorio, neither of these gentlemen
left a lasting mark on the music of their second country. Music in the
English-speaking world became very much a Sunday affair, and adjunct
to the Sunday Service, and this situation persisted in many parts of Canada well into the middle of the present century.

Things are different today, of course, as we all know. The story has
many chapters and it reaches a climax of sorts at the middle of the century and in the middle of the country, in Toronto in the years just after
the end of World War II. These were also the time and place of my own

student years, and my account is based in part on research, in part on personal recall, the one feeding the other.

The earliest Austrian musician to settle permanently in Canada was Ludwig or Louis Waizman. He was born in Salzburg in 1863, studied composition with Joseph Rheinberger, and was graduated from the Mozarteum in 1884. Following tours of Europe and Africa with the Austrian Army Band, he emigrated to Canada in 1893, settling first in Ottawa and then, after 1903, in Toronto. The *Encyclopedia of Music in Canada*, to which I am indebted for many details in this report, describes Waizman as "composer, arranger, librarian, teacher, violist, trombonist and pianist," and it is not surprising that musical versatility should have marked the long career which continued until 1951, the year of his death. Waizman is perhaps best remembered today as the teacher of three important Canadian composer-conductors. Musical versatility is a sine qua non in this demanding field, and Percy Faith, Robert Farnon and Morris Surdin learned their lessons well. The first two achieved international success as composers and arrangers in the light classical field, while Surdin became something of a specialist in the composition of music for radio plays during the heyday of that art form in Canada in the middle decades of the century.

Another early and important arrival in Toronto was the composer, violinist and conductor Luigi von Kunits. Born in Vienna in 1870, he had studied composition with Bruckner, violin with Sevcik and music history with Hanslick, in each case an unchallenged leader in his field. He knew Brahms, Goldmark and Johann Strauss, and he seems to have been generally a man of broad culture, with knowledge of languages and literature as well as music. His early career included performances as soloist in his own violin concerto in Europe and, later, appointments as concertmaster and assistant conductor to orchestras in Chicago and Pittsburg. In 1912, he was invited to join the Canadian Academy of Music in Toronto as a teacher of violin; largely for reasons of health, he accepted this rather than another, concurrent offer to become Music Director of the Philadelphia Orchestra, a position which then went to Leopold Stokowski.

The influence of von Kunits on music generally and on string playing in particular, in Toronto and throughout the rest of Canada at that time, is hard to imagine. Among his students one finds, for example, all three Adaskin brothers, Harry, the violinist, John, the cellist, conductor and impressario, and Murray, the composer. Among his many other students, Eugene Kash and Maurice Solway used their mastery of the violin as the basis of important programs of music for children, Albert Pratz was for many years a violinist in the NBC Symphony under Toscanini before to returning to Canada as a successful private teacher, and the violist Stanley Solomon continues to serve as a model for all Canadians who would take on the challenge of that most difficult of string instruments.

In 1922, von Kunits brought some of these and other Toronto musicians together to form the New Symphony Orchestra, the reincarnation of an earlier group which had been forced to disband under wartime pressure in 1918. The new group took up the old name of Toronto Symphony Orchestra in 1927 and has remained in continuous existence under that name ever since. Von Kunits served as conductor until his death in 1931, and his legacy of string playing in the Viennese tradition was the orchestra's outstanding musical quality well past the middle of the century.

Good string playing in Toronto was encouraged in those early days also by the Hambourg's, a family of Russian musicians some of whom had settled in Toronto in 1910. Boris, a gifted cellist and the most active member of the group, invited his friends Geza and Norah de Kresz (he a violinist born in 1882 in Budapest, she a pianist born in England in the same year) to join the teaching staff of the Hambourg Conservatory in 1923. Geza de Kresz had studied with both Sevcik and Ysaye and had held a series of distinguished court appointments and presigious orchestral chairs throughout Central Europe, including, from 1917 through 1921, that of concertmaster of the Berlin Philharmonic. The de Kresz's were active in Toronto until 1935. They then spent the period 1935 to 1947 in Europe, where Geza served as President of the National Conservatory in Budapest. In 1947, they returned to Toronto and remained there until Geza's death in 1959; Norah died six months later in Budapest. Through all these wanderings, they kept alive their contacts with musicians in all parts of Europe; for Canadians who knew them well, they were a rich source of knowledge about all that was great, and also much that could be sad, about a life in music.

As a teacher, Geza de Kresz may have influenced a smaller number of students than von Kunits, but that influence may also have been deeper and longer lasting. One of his early students in Toronto was Clayton Hare, a Canadian violinist of great distinction who in turn became the first teacher of three of the finest string players this country has yet produced, Francis Chaplin, Andrew Dawes (leader of the Orford Quartet), and Betty-Jean Hagen. The last of these studied also with de Kresz in the forties and fifties and herself had a successful international career.

Another of de Kresz's Canadian students was Adolf Koldofsky, who later moved to Los Angeles and became friends with the Viennese expatriate composer Arnold Schoenberg; the "Fantasy," opus 47, for Violin and Piano, Schoenberg's last composition, was written for Koldofsky and dedicated to him.

In 1924, the year after his arrival in Toronto, Geza de Kresz founded the Hart House String Quartet, Canada's first fully subsidized chamber ensemble. The group took its name from that of the theatre where the first concert took place, and the Massey Foundation, which had earlier financed Hart House as a gift to the University of Toronto, became the chief financial support of the Quartet as well. The group remained in existence for over twenty years, playing a broadly varied repertoire ranging from standard literature to first performances, and in many important ways setting a fine standard for the many groups that would follow.

All this string playing was supported by the presence in Toronto, from 1912, of George Heinl, a violin maker and dealer in string instruments born in Austria in 1891. Serving at first as the Canadian representative of the prestigious London firm of Hill & Sons, Heinl eventually opened his own business in Toronto in 1926, passing control to his son in 1944. George Heinl & Co. is now run by the founder's grandson and remains an important part of the Toronto musical scene.

Von Kunits' successor as conductor of the Toronto Symphony was a fortyish Toronto organist of Scottish extraction named Ernest Campbell MacMillan, a broadly gifted musician of equally well-honed political instincts. He remained at the post for twenty-five years and was, during the thirties and early forties, the best known and most influential musician in English-speaking Canada. To a sometimes ridiculous degree, he became the public embodiment of Canada's musical life. A man of many parts, Sir Ernest (as he became in 1935) was the Canadian establishment musician who best understood the musical traditions of continental Europe, and as such was an important pivotal figure in much of what follows.

When the Viennese Lieder singer Emmi Heim visited Canada in 1934, she found in Sir Ernest an artist of musical tastes very like her own and, in time, a warm personal friend. She continued to come to Canada for extended periods throughout the thirties and settled permanently in Toronto at war's end. In her teaching, which continued until a matter of weeks before her death in 1954, she became for her students a living and vibrant exemplar of all that was true, beautiful and good in Viennese art and life.

Emmi Heim was born in Vienna in 1885. Following her debut there in 1911, she toured widely throughout the Empire, in Germany and Poland, and in England where she lived from 1930. Her repertoire included songs not only of Schubert, Schumann and Hugo Wolf but also of composers who were among her contemporaries and acquaintances—Schoenberg, Berg, Stravinsky, the musical "bad boys" of her time. She also had a great sensitivity for what was then the modern French repertory, songs by Fauré and Duparc and Chausson and Debussy. Her circle of acquaintances did not stop with musicians and composers. She had known Rilke and Hofmannsthal, Kokoschka had done her portrait; when the Metropolitan Opera came to town, Rudolf Bing came to call. It seemed to us that Emmi (as we all called her) had known anyone who mattered.

Emmi Heim brought to her teaching the colourful variety of a kaleioscope focused with intensity of a laser beam. Vocal technique as such had no place in her pantheon. Personality, yes, but also a searing study of the meaning of the text, of what the text meant to the composer and how this was reflected in the music, of what the text and the music meant to the singer, and of how all this was to be conveyed to the listener. The greatest sin was to let escape even a single note that was not invested with maximum expression. It was a regimen that no student ever forgot.

During the late thirties, Central European musicians began arriving in Toronto in greater numbers. While they enriched the scene by their presence, their moment of major influence came only after the war, by which time the social climate became more conducive to change, the immigrants (as they were sometimes called derisively) had acquired a deeper understanding of their new home, and they were joined by others who, like themselves, had brought to Canada their lives, their rich and varied backgrounds—and little else.

By far the most important of these late-thirties arrivals was Arnold Walter, a composer, pianist and cultural polymath born in Moravia in 1902. A man of enormous erudition, a true son of the Empire with a keen sense of history, he once described his early education as "a 17th century prescription for 20th century youngsters." He was one of those persons who might properly be described as addicted to learning. History and literature were his hobbies and he used to read himself to sleep in Latin and Greek. At his father's insistence he completed a law degree at Prague University, but his real interests lay elsewhere—in the piano (which he studied with Frederic Lamond), in music composition (one of his teachers was

Franz Schreker, an important but nearly forgotten opera and symphonic composer of the time) and in music history (the legendary Curt Sachs was an important influence). His career as a music journalist in Berlin was abruptly terminated by political developments of 1933; without even packing his bags, he took the next train for Paris, then spent three lean years on the Island of Majorca and a year in London. In 1937, he was appointed to the staff of Upper Canada College in Toronto as a teacher of history, and there he remained for seven long years—though, as might be expected, he was far from being idle after school! We shall meet him again at war's end.

Walter's arrival in Toronto was followed a year later by that of Greta Kraus, a harpsichordist of distinction who was born in Vienna in 1907 and left there in a great hurry in 1938. She was one of the few certifiable students of the Viennese music theorist Heinrich Schenker, a man whose name is now common coin in every music school in North America. She brought to Canada a depth of understanding and appreciation for the harpsichord and its music that might not otherwise have come for many years. She was the regular continuo player in MacMillan's annual performances of Bach's "St. Matthew Passion," she founded and played for many years with the Toronto Baroque Ensemble, and she taught many younger harpsichordists the secrets of her art. In a parallel career, which continues to this day, she has coached many singers in the fine points of Austrian German and Viennese singing style.

Two other important musicians from the Empire arrived in Canada in 1940 and remain active to the present time. The pianist Lubka Kolessa was born in 1902 in Lviv, Galicia, then (under the name Lemberg) very much a part of Franz Joseph's dominion, and moved with her family to Vienna in early childhood; she studied with two eminent students of Franz Liszt, Emil Sauer and Eugen d'Albert, and enjoyed a successful solo career before leaving Europe. Oskar Morawetz, a prolific composer born in what was later called Czechoslovakia in 1917, had already attracted favourable attention in Prague and Vienna for his score-reading skills as a pianist before moving with his family to Toronto at the age of 23; he continues to enrich Canada's musical landscape as both a composer and teacher, not least in his many sensitive settings of texts by Canadian poets.

With the end of the war, Toronto's musical life entered a period of unmatched growth and change. This revolution (for such it was) began as a series of curriculum reforms at the Royal Conservatory of Music and, a little later, in the Faculty of Music at the University of Toronto. The chief architect and driving force behind these changes was Arnold Walter, who had moved at war's end into a position of power within the Conservatory and would later take over as Director of the Faculty. Walter's actions were not universally admired, his methods were not always tactful, and his path was often blocked by those who had felt the weight of his steps on their toes. Things were not made easier by the fact that his command of the English language, impeccable and even colourful though it could be on paper, left something to be desired in the speaking; his speech was graced with a Central European lilt of indeterminate origin, and this habit sat ill on the ears of those who had suffered loss in two European wars. In a word, Walter was anti-establishment, and even the politic Ernest MacMillan was not always to be found on his side of an issue. Yet somehow he got the job done, and somehow he managed to stay in the saddle.

One of Walter's earliest reforms was to set up an opera school, an action he took in 1946. As music director he brought in Nicholas Goldschmidt, a man of many talents, born in Moravia in 1908. Goldschmidt studied composition, piano and voice at the Vienna Academy of Music, where one of his fellow students was Herbert von Karajan, and filled several conducting posts in Czechoslovakia and Belgium before moving to the United States in 1937. During his American years, he taught opera the San Francisco Conservatory and at Stanford and Columbia Universities. He thus brought a wealth of gifts and background to his Toronto post, and he attacked his new duties with characteristic energy and enthusiasm. In 1948, Goldschmidt was joined by the German-born opera stage director Herman Geiger-Torel, with whom he had worked years before in Czechoslovakia, and together these two volatile friends built a grand operatic edifice.

The success of the opera school was really quite phenomenol. Singers came from all over the country, drawn by the prospect of good teaching and training, leading to professional engagements. In 1948, the CBC formed its own opera company to give radio productions; Torel, Goldschmidt and Walter were all active in the initial stages of this enterprise, as was Geoffrey Waddington, another von Kunits student now become de facto head of music for CBC. Casting relied heavily on the presence of students at the school, who thereby were given a first chance to display their vocal talents to a wider world. By 1950, the school had given birth to a professional company which mounted an annual season in Toronto and, from 1958, sent touring productions coast-to-coast under its new name of Canadian Opera Company. Repertoire ran the gamut from late Mozart to the latest by Harry Somers. And supportive of all this public activity was the fine voice teaching going on behind the scenes in the studios of Emmi Heim (until 1954), Greta Kraus and, after 1952, the Viennese-born and internationally acclaimed dramatic soprano Irene Jessner.

Yet another important Austrian musician enters the story at this point: Franz Kraemer, born in Vienna in 1914 and, while still in his teens, a composition student of Alban Berg. Kraemer was one of those hundreds of German-speaking Europeans who made their way to England prior to 1940, only to be swept up by the British Government and transported to a cold and far-off place. Having spent much of the war in political incarceration, Kraemer made his way to Toronto where he studied briefly with Arnold Walter and then, in 1946, joined the CBC International Service in Montreal as a producer. In 1952, he returned to Toronto as an executive producer for CBC-TV and became an important pioneer in the production of opera for television. In this and in his later role as music officer of the Canada Council, using a well informed imagination and quiet persistence, Kraemer brought a creative dimension to the growth Canada's musical scene.

One finds the CBC nearly everywhere in this account of the burgeoning musical life of Canada at mid-century. CBC support of music was not limited to the production of opera; there were CBC studio orchestras in half-a-dozen cities, and the corporation consistently picked up for broadcast the live concerts given by public orchestras in larger centres. From 1952 to 1964, the CBC maintained in Toronto, under the musical and administrative guidance of Geoffrey Waddington, a large orchestra of such quality as to attract the favourable attention of Igor Stravinsky and his associate, Robert Craft, who recorded with that orchestra for Columbia Records in the early sixties.

At a time when the CBC finds itself under constant political attack, it might be well to ask how all this musical largesse came about. There is no evidence of enlightened Austrian immigrants in the top echelons of CBC management. Neither, for that matter, was there a ministry of culture in the federal cabinet, and this is perhaps a clue. There was no Canada Council in the mid-fifties; while growth in the arts was widely recognized, no government at any level had yet found the political courage to extend direct support from the public coffers to activities seen by many as frivolous. The Massey Commission on Arts, Letters and Sciences had urged, in its report of 1951, that some such funding body be set up at the federal level, but the government, searching in vain for a groundswell of broad public support, waited until 1957 before putting in place the agency we all know as the keystone of arts support in the years since. There is a case to be made, then, that all this musical activity on the CBC, not to mention a parallel river of radio and television drama, may have been by way of a sort of hidden subsidy, pending the day when direct support might become politically more feasible.

The lack of political will to support the arts showed itself in another way at about this time, in the city of Toronto the Good, and here it can be said that the long arm of Viennese musical culture may have had a small hand in the outcome. It should be borne in mind that the social life of Toronto in the mid-fifties was still largely governed by restrictive laws which even a genuine Victorian would have found—well, Victorian. Much of Ontario was still "dry" and some church leaders found it impossible to distinguish between a performing arts venue and a den of iniquity. Nothing was open on Sunday, not even a movie theatre, and Toronto was universally known for its "blue laws." A European wit of the time proposed a competition offering, as first prize, a week in Toronto; the second prize was to be two weeks in Toronto.

It was in this social atmosphere that some one suggested, in the early weeks of 1955, that the Toronto City Council should fund a Civic Centre for the Arts. To say that support for such a proposal was soft would be an understatement; outside the arts community, there was virtually no support at all. Into this political vacuum stepped E.P. Taylor, a prominent business tycoon and horse lover of the time. Speaking through the president of one of his companies, Taylor offered to build a theatre if the city would supply the land. The company was a brewery and the resulting uproar may be hard to imagine in this day and age. Yet there were those who thought the city should not look a gift horse in the mouth, so to speak.

As it happened, the Canadian Opera Company was about to open a run of Johann Strauss' "Die Fledermaus" at the height of this brouhaha. The plot of this Viennese concoction centres around an attempt to amuse the immensely wealthy but hopelessly bored Prince Orlovsky, and traditon dictates that Orlovsky's Song, which falls at the mid-point of Act II, should have a second verse added with local and topical content. Well, here is what the Canadian Opera Company gave Orlovsky to sing on that momentous occasion:

Although I've travelled round the world and been most everywhere,
Toronto on a Sunday night is more than I can bear.
The bars and theatres all are closed, the cinema is taboo.
The library and the zoo, they might as well be too.

If I were mayor for just one day, you'd get a big surprise,
A civic centre I'd construct, in spite of all the "drys."
And if some one objected, you know what he could do!
It is Orlovsky's custom: "Chaqu'un à son gout."

Well, as we all know, the O'Keefe Centre did get built and Toronto is no longer a boring place on Sunday nights or any other time, and if some part of the credit falls to Austrian immigrants, so be it!

I have always thought it a privilege to have been around during those years of maximum Central European influence on our musical life. The magic of it all was enhanced for me by the fact that, during my childhood, during the worst years of the war, anything having to do with Central European values was effectively blocked from our ready acceptance by clever propaganda, much of it based in ridicule, with the result that this festive spread of new and wonderful sounds and ideas provoked a reaction akin to addiction. We didn't just listen to all that great music; we studied it, we performed it, we challenged our teachers to tell us what it all meant, we squeezed them like lemons for everything they had to offer. What they must have thought of some of us I cannot imagine but I never heard from any of them a single word of complaint, neither about their new estate nor about whatever they had been forced to leave behind. For four years I studied composition with Arnold Walter, for three years I was Emmi Heim's studio accompanist, for two years I accompanied rehearsals at the opera school, and it was generously arranged that, for one long year, including two summers in Salzburg, I was a student in Europe. May I be forgiven for believing that my student days were an important time for the enrichment of Canada's musical life?

I think the record will support my belief. Let me touch briefly on the careers of some of those who were students either with me or in the years just before or after. Among singers, I can count at least eleven who achieved international renown: Victor Braun, Mark DuBois, Robert Goulet, Lois Marshall, Roxolana Roslak, Jan Rubes, Teresa Stratas, Lilian Sukis, Jon Vickers and Jeannette Zarou. These were all "products of the opera school" as also was Bernard Turgeon, who crowned a successful performing career by creating the role of Louis Riel in Harry Somers' opera and then went on to a long and successful teaching career at the Universities of Alberta and Victoria and at McGill. The opera school also "produced" the conductor Mario Bernardi, long the Music Director of the National Arts Centre Orchestra and later of the CBC Vancouver Chamber Orchestra and the Calgary Philharminic; and the opera stage director Irving Guttman, the founding Artistic Director of the Vancouver Opera and, since 1965, the Artistic Director of the Edmonton Opera.

Among pianists who studied with Kolessa around my time, several have had long and distinguished performing and teaching careers. These include Howard Brown at Bishop's University, Gordon Kushner at the Royal Conservatory in Toronto, John Hawkins at the University of Toronto, Louis-Philippe Pelletier at McGill, and Clermont Pepin at the Conservatoire de musique du Québec à Montréal. Both Brown and Pepin also count Arnold Walter as an important teacher, the one for music history, the other for composition.

Of course, Walter's curriculum reforms did not begin and end with the opera school. From the early fifties, he introduced new degree programs within the Faculty of Music at the University of Toronto. In these he largely followed an emerging American pattern whereby the practical, theoretical and humanistic aspects of music education would all be taught within the university. To put it another way, he recognized that the freestanding music school or independent conservatory had an uncertain role to play in the future of North American society, and that the university would have to carry the full burden if music was to have a place in the lives of Canadians. While this approach makes music education at the university level a bit of a round peg in a square hole, it has become the model for other universities in English-speaking Canada and has given music a firmer place in Canadian life than it would otherwise have had.

The place of music in society was something of an *idée fixe* with Walter. At the very end of his life, he was attempting to assemble his thoughts on the subject in book form. Work in this field has been carried on in practical terms by yet another of his students, Helmut Kallmann, who was born in Berlin in 1922, arrived in Canada as an incarcerated alien in 1940, and was made Chief of the newly formed Music Division of the National Library of Canada in 1970. From that high office and also as editor-in-chief of both editions of the *Encyclopedia of Music in Canada*, in his many writings on Canada's music, in his appearances as visiting lecturer at many Canadian universities, in his contributions to international reference works, and in many, many other ways Kallmann, following in Walter's footsteps, has given Canada the basis of a much needed sense of its own music history.

The Austrian-inspired enrichment of Canada's musical life continued well after mid-century, then, and not only through education and the dissemination of ideas. From 1957 to 1962, Nicholas Goldschmidt was artistic and managing director of the Vancouver International Festival, a series of high profile events that brought new standards of musical and artistic expression to that city. A major supporter of the Festival was the Koerner Foundation, named after a family of Czech refugees who had prospered in timber after moving to British Columbia in 1939. In a sense, Goldschmidt may be said to have found a new career as impresario, for he later became successively chief of the performing arts division of the Centennial Commission, artistic director of the Guelph Spring Festival, consultant to the Algoma Fall Festival in Sault Ste. Marie, and director to a veritable feast of festivals in and around Toronto. At this writing he is preparing a production of Britten's church opera "Noye's Fludde" in celebration of the fiftieth anniversary of the founding of the United Nations in June.

Other Austrian musicians have come and gone and some have stayed. Alfred Rose, the son of Gustav Mahler's sister, lived in London, Ontario from 1948 and did much pioneering work in the arcane discipline of music therapy prior to his death in 1975. Among Sir Ernest MacMillan's successors on the podium of the Toronto Symphony were two Czech's born subjects of Franz Joesph, Walter Susskind and Karel Ancerl. Sonia Eckhardt-Gramatté, an immensely gifted composer, pianist and violinist, accompanied her husband Ferdinand Eckhardt, an art historian of Austrian birth, when he became director of the Winnipeg Art Gallery in 1953; the E-Gre Competition for the Performance of Canadian Music, a project in planning during her last years, was held for the first time only after her sudden death in 1974. The musicologist Ida Halpern, born in Vienna in 1910, conducted valuable field research in the music of Canada's west coast Indian groups between her arrival in Vancouver in 1939 and her death there in 1987. There have been many others: the historian Willy Amtmann, the conductors Agnes Grossman and Georg Tintner, the guitarists Eli Kassner and Norbert Kraft, the pianist Anton Kuerti, the composer Gerhard Wuensch—the Austrian presence in music is everywhere.

Yet I shall always remember those ten magical, turbulent years when all the wealth and beauty of a millenium was injected, or so it seemed, into the bloodstream of a still raw and culturally undeveloped country. And whenever I think of those times and those events, I think also of Rilke's wonderful line: "*Denn so war es noch nie.*"

VIII

THE HISTORY OF THE EGGER FAMILY
OF IMMIGRANTS TO CANADA

*Thomas Samhaber*
*St. Martin, Austria*


THE STORY OF THE EGGER FAMILY and their immigration to Canada is in many ways a special case, but it touches on many of the general themes of our broader theme of Austrian immigration to Canada. The story which follows is based a number of German letters written between 1905 and 1948, which total more than 80 pages in all. Only the letters sent from Canada to Austria still exist. The responses have regrettably been lost. Nevertheless the basic outline of this family's migration can be reconstructed from these letters, and much valuable information on the Austrian immigration experience can be gleaned from them. The following brief excerpts present some highlights from this correspondence.[1]

At the turn of the century the Egger family was one of the most respected families in the region surrounding Bruck near Peuerbach. Ever since the seventeenth century they had been the owners of a so-called *"Meierhof,"* or large farm, in this village in the province of Upper Austria. Leopold Egger was 14 years old when he had to take over the farm in 1885, after his parents had died of typhus. Two years later he founded the first brick-factory in this area, and in 1888 he married a girl from a nearby town, the 20-year-old Elisabeth Achleitner. In the first five years of their marriage four sons were born: Siegfried, Theodor, Albrecht and Friedrich. At some stage during these years the Eggers decided to emigrate to the United States, and in 1904 they began to buy land in California.

The motives behind this decision to emigrate are difficult to discern. There are no comments about it in their subsequent letters. It appeared to have been a quick decision and it came as a real surprise to most of the other inhabitants of Peuerbach. But because the reasons remained a mystery, people speculated on a number of possibilities. It may have been that the brick-factory did not develop as well as Leopold expected. Reports from America might have awoken his interest. A relative who had already emigrated may have served as a role model. It seems likely that the young farmer and entrepreneur was interested in cheap land and modern mechanical farming methods in North America. One of the details we do know is that on the family's subsequent voyage from California to Saskatchewan, the Eggers made a major detour just to see a farming machines fair.

Two passages in subsequent letters seem to indicate that the personal alienation Elisabeth Egger felt in Peuerbach played some role in the decision to emigrate. Coming from a town, small though it may have been, she never really felt comfortable in the rural surroundings of Bruck near Peuerbach. She made no secret of it, when she wrote from Canada: "I thought that we were now far enough away from Peuerbach, so that people could not talk about us any more, but still they are gossiping."[2] When she discovered that one of her friends from the area had also moved away, she commented:

I am so pleased for her from the bottom of my heart, that she has been able to get away from that awful hole, Bruck. We certainly have not regretted being away from this agonizing tribulation for a single day. Only now do we realize how many sorrows and pain we had there, and how good we have it here.[3]

Only a few weeks before the family's emigration a daughter, who was named Frieda, was born to Elisabeth. Given the potential vicissitudes of the long voyage, the family decided to leave the new-born baby with Leopold's brother Franz Egger and his wife Maria, who had no children of their own and could well afford to raise her. Leopold and Elisabeth planned to have their daughter brought over to America when she was older, and in the meantime little Frieda went to live with her uncle, Franz, the owner of an inn, in his villa in Peuerbach.

Following the example of a relative, the Eggers first went to San Francisco and settled on their land in California. After a while, however, they began to realize that the warm climate was extremely detrimental to Leopold's health. Following the advice of a doctor, who recommended a change of climate, they left California for British Columbia. Arriving after a long train journey through Portland and Seattle, they discovered that a suitable piece of land was impossible to find. At this point they read in a local newspaper that good and cheap land was available further east. Boarding the Canadian Pacific Railway they travelled to Regina and finally came came to Prince Albert. Approaching the prior of the bishop there to inquire where he could buy land, Leopold found that he could get a quarter section of virgin land from the Canadian government for free. This is how the Egger family came to settle in Dead Moose Lake, in the area of Pilger near Humboldt, Saskatchewan.

The initial problems were no doubt enormous. The journey with four little children had been hard, savings were exhausted, and what money was still due from their sold possessions in Austria came irregularly and in too small installments. In 1905 Leopold wrote to his brother:

This is to let you know that I have received the 500 Gulden, and I can let you know at the same time that with such a small amount of money it is impossible to make a start here. Our Austrian money vanishes here too quickly.... We have written Dr. Ritter in Wels asking him to send us 1200 Gulden.... Please go to him and tell him to send this money immediately.... Because winter is approaching and we still have to build a house and a stable before then. Then we have to buy some cattle to be able to get through the winter. Don't delay a single day, for you cannot imagine how difficult it is to be in a foreign country without money.[4]

During these first years in Canada another son, named Leopold, and two daughters, Elsie and Marianne (called Mary), were born in quick succession.

In their third year in Canada Leopold began to suffer from terrible headaches. Doctors once more prescribed a change of climate, and the family therefore decided to return to Austria. They began preparations for the return journey and had already sold a part of their land when Leopold suddenly died, 14 days before the planned departure date. Elisabeth Egger was left completely on her own with seven children. She was never able to collect the money for the land they had sold. Writing to her daughter in Austria about this episode some years later, she noted

When your real father died we were very poor, because he had sold everything, and wanted to go back to Austria. The people who bought our land could never afford to pay and so I lost the money. It was under such circumstances, with only two cows and some chickens, that I had to feed myself and your seven siblings for two-and-a-half years. You can well imagine all the things I had to go through and that all this was not very easy for me.[5]

In February 1911, two and a half years after Leopold's death, Elisabeth remarried. Her second husband was a local farmer named Johann Loose, with whom she had four more children: Joe, Henry, Antonius (who died in infancy) and Pauline. Together with the sons from her first marriage they managed to cultivate and enlarge the farm. As the sons and daughters grew up, they settled in the neighbourhood, and most of them became farmers as well.

Of particular interest are those parts of the letters which Elisabeth sent to Austria in which she compared her old home with her new one in Canada. In 1910, for example, she wrote:

The three oldest [children] always say: mother, we will never go back to Austria. We don't want to serve in the army. We can earn more money here than there. Siegfried in particular is very ambitious for money.... I always say it would probably be better for me in Austria but better for the boys here. There, every boy can go to a pub and get drunk, but here no boy under 18 is able to get any alcoholic beverage. Woe to the bar owner who does it, for he is immediately fined $200. That is something I like better about this place than there [in Austria]. One never knows if [the boys] will all turn out well, and there I would not be able to keep them with me—they would have to seek employment with strangers. But here they can stay at home and work diligently.[6]

In another letter she wrote:

The way of living was and is much better here than in Austria. In this country it is like this: first you make sure that you have things that you like on your table, and what is left over is sold. But there [in Austria] we had to sell everything. Fruit doesn't grow here, but you can still get everything because it is imported.[7]

One point always stressed in the letters was that the young sons were able to get better wages in Canada:

Albert is with a farmer who has 320 acres of land, and this is worked by only two men, the farmer and Albert. The wages are also very high here. Siegfried as well as Thedi get $80 a month, Albert gets $70. That's an awful lot of money. The farm work is done with machines.[8]

Elisabeth's children grew up bilingually. There was a school in the area which could be attended for at least half of the year. As one letter points out:

Siegfried, Thedi, Albrecht and Friedrich went to school for the whole summer. They had six months of school; now it is over. In winter it's too cold here. We get down to 45 degrees below zero, and with such temperatures you can't let the children outdoors. I'm always sorry that the children have to miss so much time at school. When they are at school they learn well. They learn German and English.[9]

In the schools the children visited after they had moved closer to town, they seem to have had no more German lessons.

Poldi, Elsa and Marie and your stepbrother Josef go to school, but they learn everything in English. But at home only German is spoken so that the children don't unlearn it.[10]

The correspondence between Elisabeth Egger and her relatives and friends in Peuerbach lasted about half a century. Now and then they also heard from each other through friends from Austria who also immigrated to Canada.

It was a great comfort for me when Anton Zehetmayr arrived here because we could talk about many things which cannot be written about in letters. I think it took us a whole week to talk over all the news.[11]

Of course, the most important focus in Elisabeth's letters is her daughter, whom she had to leave behind. Inquiries about her daughter dominate every letter, as, for example, this one from 1905: "How is our dear Frieda? Is she already big and strong? We are looking forward to your letter, to hear about our little child. Our sweethearts here often ask about Frieda."[12] Frieda herself, however, only learned the details of her parentage when she was 15 years old, and her foster-parents, Franz and Maria Egger, told her the whole story. At that point mother and daughter began to exchange letters.

My dear Frieda!
I received your lovely letter with the pictures, and I thank you dearly for it. I can see from the photo that you are already big and strong and well educated.... Whenever I see your picture I am always very moved that wretched fate has separated us. Now, dear Frieda, I hope God will grant that we can see each other once more.[13]

Elisabeth had promised her husband Leopold at his deathbed that she would bring Frieda to Canada. In the following years it became more and more unrealistic to keep this promise. Elisabeth, for her part, frequently talked about coming back to Austria, but it never happened.

When Frieda married Josef Samhaber in 1926, the couple thought of spending their honeymoon in Canada with her mother. But the plan fell through, largely because of Elisabeth's concern for the financial implications:

That would be very nice, but it will cost you a lot of money, which neither you nor we have. We also still do not have any savings, because such a big family as ours costs a lot of money, and everything is expensive here. The return trip would cost you almost $1,000 dollars, if you count all the money you would need in addition to the fares. It is better to keep the money that you have and set up a nice home with it.... The best thing is to leave things as they are now, and one day we will certainly meet.[14]

In fact, mother and daughter never did meet again, for in the year 1942 Frieda Samhaber died unexpectedly at the age of 38.

The brothers were also anxious to see their sister once again, and some of the letters were exchanges between Frieda and her brothers. The boys often wrote their sister in Austria, but it is evident that their image of the old country became increasingly cliché-ridden. For example, one letter contained an inquiry about a prospective Austrian bride: "For now we are still single, but I don't want to stay that way too much longer. I've already got a miss on the line. Albert wants to get one from Austria. Why don't you find one for him. A beautiful one who is good at yodeling."[15]

Political subjects almost never arose in these letters, and even the world wars were only alluded to in connection with perceived rising prices: "Since the war," Elisabeth wrote her daughter in 1919, "prices have gone up horribly. From your letter I see it is even worse with you [in Austria]. A good pair of nice shoes now cost ten dollars!"[16] During the war itself, of course, correspondence was very difficult. Letters from Austria were sent to a relative in Minnesota, who then forwarded them to Saskatchewan. The exchange, however, was sporadic, much to the distress of Elisabeth:

My heart can barely stand trying once again to write a few lines to you, my dear ones. I wrote some letters to you, and got not one in return. Postal connections are very bad. But you must not think, that we have forgotten you—no—we speak about you every day. It must be quite frightful with the war.[17]

Political events in Germany and Austria during the 1930s, and especially the rise of Hitler obviously made the Eggers' relationships with their neighbours difficult, as the following letter of 1938 shows:

You write that business is going better now than before. Dear Juli, I have to ask you if it is really true what people here say about Hittler [sic]. They say that he is visciously against religion. Is that true? Please answer this question in your next letter, so I can shut them up. You know how it is, there are always people like that everywhere, for whom nothing that is done is ever good enough.[18]

As Elisabeth's children grew up, she began to report their successes proudly: "Thedi, Friedrich and Leopold are big farmers. Each one has his own car, and they do their farming with machines. Everything is done on a large scale."[19] Friedrich (Frederick) Egger and Albert settled in the same area as their parents:

We have now been in Lake Lenore for one year. It is a small town by a lake, which has sprung up virtually over night. One year ago Lake Lenore was no more than a village with an auxiliary church with rectory, a little store and few farm-houses. Then the railway came, and immediately a little town with four big grain elevators, ... a bank, five shops, one drug store, two pool-halls, two gas stations, etc., emerged.[20]

In 1947 the now already 79-year-old Elisabeth wrote:

The children are all grown up, and they are all on their own now. Each has their own home, and they are all doing well. My husband and I are now alone. We bought ourselves a little house in Marysburg, next to the church, where we have a very comfortable life. All our children live in the vicinity and they visit us often.[21]

Elisabeth Egger Loose died at the age of 88 in 1956 and is buried at Humboldt, Saskatchewan.

The correspondence between the Austrian and Canadian branches of this family did not end with her death. Relatives on both sides of the Atlantic have visited each other often. In 1984 Frieda's daughter Herta toured Canada with her own son, Markus. Along the way they visited all of Frieda's surviving brothers and sisters, as well as seventy other relatives. Good connections have already been established, and it appears likely that Elisabeth's six Austrian great-grandchildren will one day get together with her eighty Canadian ones.

# ENDNOTES

1. All letters quoted are from the author's private collection.
2. Elisabeth Egger to Franz, Maria and Frieda Egger, 1910.
3. Elisabeth Egger to Mrs. Payer, 1915.
4. Leopold Egger to Franz and Maria Egger, 1905.
5. Elisabeth Egger to Frieda Egger, 1924.
6. Elisabeth Egger to Franz, Maria and Frieda Egger, 1910.
7. Elisabeth Egger to Frieda Egger, 1919.
8. Elisabeth Egger to Frieda Egger, 1919.
9. Elisabeth Egger to Julie Egger-Fischer, 1909.
10. Elisabeth Egger to Franz and Maria Egger, 1927, and Elisabeth Egger to Frieda Egger, 1919.
11. Elisabeth Egger to Franz and Maria Egger, 1927.
12. Leopold Egger to Franz and Maria Egger, 1905.
13. Elisabeth Egger to Frieda Egger, 1919.
14. Elisabeth Egger to Josef Samhaber, 1924.
15. Frederik and Albert Egger to Frieda Egger, 1922.
16. Elisabeth Egger to Frieda Egger, 1919.
17. Elisabeth Egger to Maria Egger, 1916.
18. Elisabeth Egger to Julie Egger-Fischer, 1927.
19. Elisabeth Egger to Julie Egger-Fischer, 1948.
20. Frederik and Albert Egger to Frieda Egger, 1922.
21. Elisabeth Egger to Julie Egger-Fischer, 1948.

IX

## IMMIGRATION: A PERSONAL RETROSPECTIVE
## OF AN AUSTRIAN IN CANADA

*Helmut Walter Ott*
*University of New Brunswick*

MY MEMORIES OF IMMIGRATION are multi-faceted: a kaleidoscope of new experiences, fresh impressions, and turbulent emotional upheavals. In this essay I try to create a background to those memories and link what happened to me with a corresponding inner reconstruction and development of my person. Physical relocation from one country to another is quickly accomplished. The personal adjustments, the psychological reconstructions, of cultural relocation take significantly longer to stabilize. In my own case it took many years.

I was born in 1944 in Koflach, Austria. My mother had moved there to give birth to me because during the war her home town of Graz was no longer safe from frequent bombing attacks. I arrived in Canada in early May 1953, after a long boat trip aboard the Italian liner, *Vulcania*. I was 8 years old and came with my mother and brother who was two years older than me. My father left Austria the year before to find a job and a place for us to live. His brother, my uncle, had preceded him to the new world the year before that. My uncle's letters contained glowing descriptions of Canadian life. These, no doubt, encouraged my father to emigrate also.

I often try to establish the main causes for my parents' leaving Austria. Was it only for economic reasons? My father was an artistic engraver and jewellery maker who found little work in post-war Austria. He dreamed of having his own business, buying a car, and enjoying a comfortable life. Or was it the political uncertainty of post-war Austria? Vienna remained occupied by Russia whose soldiers left a legacy of fear. Many

Austrian women were abused by Russians in the latter stages of the Second World War. My mother told us frightening stories: how she hid from Russian soldiers scouring southern Styria; how young women and children could not consider themselves safe whenever Russians were around; how homes were looted and resistors shot. These stories left a permanent imprint on my mind. I remember in 1952 our crossing by streetcar the Russian sector of Vienna to get our visa and emigration papers for Canada. Fear filled us as we neared the barbed-wire check point. Everyone on the streetcar had to get off and be interrogated by uniformed Russian soldiers before being allowed to proceed. I was really scared. These are early memory fragments for me. I honestly do not know the main reason why our family left. At any rate, my parents said we would come to Canada for only five years and then return home with lots of money and total fluency in English.

Leaving Austria, and my home town of Graz, was not easy. Even now, the memories surrounding separation bring with them feelings of sadness. As a child I was very close to my grandparents and close to my friends. I had completed the first three grades in the *Nibelungenvolksschule* and felt very much at home in my neighbourhood. Though our parents forbade us to go there, among the fascinating play areas I remember were the piles of rubble and numerous bombed out buildings left after the war. As children, we used to play cops and robbers in those bunkers because they provided great hiding places. The countryside around Graz was lovely. In the summer our grandparents frequently took us to the surrounding woods to pick mushrooms; in the fall, we searched for chestnuts. I was very close to my grandparents. My brother and I were their only grandchildren as my mother was their only child. In a nutshell, I had close friends, a home, and a sense of belonging. Life felt totally complete for me, perfect and happy. The thought of leaving Graz was a jolting intrusion which I put out of my mind for as long as I could.

Nevertheless, as the departure date crept closer final farewells with acquaintances increased, as did promises never to forget one another. The shadow of leaving eventually fell across all our daily activities. In the last few days we visited my grandparents daily. I can still see them watching from their second storey window, waiting to see my brother and me getting off the street car. We liked to visit Oma and Opa. But those final days were sad. Opa and Oma seemed quiet and downcast. They would look at us with an empty stare for long periods of time. Eventually their eyes would brim with tears and Oma would repeat, "Why must you go *so* far away? Stay here. Things will soon get better. Stay home; otherwise we are all alone." My brother and I tried to lighten the situation. We reassured them we would only be gone for a little while.

My father had written encouraging letters from Canada. His clinching argument in each letter was the promise that when we came to Montreal my brother and I would find a room filled with all the toys imaginable. This promise, more than anything, fuelled us with a desire and determination to come to Canada at all costs.

When the moment of departure finally came, my grandparents and mother wept openly. I felt a lump in my throat saying goodbye. My brother and I tried not to cry. Suitcases in hand, the three of us took leave of Oma and Opa's apartment. We must have been a sorry sight with those big suitcases as we descended the staircase to the street and waited for a streetcar going to the train station. Opa and Oma said they did not want to come and see us off because it would be unbearable for them. From the street, my brother, my mother and I waved a last good bye to the tearful faces in the second storey window and then boarded the streetcar to the train station. Surprisingly, the first people we saw at there were Oma and Opa. They had taken a taxi in order to see us one final time. It was already late afternoon and before long, after another round of tearful goodbyes, we felt the train's forward motion. As it picked up speed we continued to look and wave from the open window. My final memory is grandfather standing close beside grandmother, waving a white handkerchief: two receding figures in a dimming light. The train turned a corner and they were gone.

On the train, my mother continued to cry silently and attracted the attention and sympathy of others in the compartment. So my brother and I tried to distract her. We reassured her "We would soon be back." We really had no idea of how very, very far we were about to travel. That night the train took us from Austria across the border into Italy. When we awoke the next morning we could see a landscape of steep mountain valleys and old stone bridges spanning deep ravines. Lush vegetation and tropical palm trees became more plentiful as the seaport town of Genoa, our destination and point of embarkation, came into view. From Genoa, the boat charted a two day voyage through the Mediterranean Sea stopping at various ports (Naples, Palermo) to pick up passengers. After two days, it passed by the Rock of Gibraltar and we found ourselves heading into the Atlantic Ocean, leaving the land mass of Europe behind. For seven days we saw only the open sea. When finally we noticed land again it was the coastline of Canada. What jubilation when the boat docked in Halifax and we could get off!

Emptying the boat of its two thousand passengers took a whole day. I remember vividly how Canadian immigration officials had set out large barrels which they kept filling with confiscated Italian salamis, cheeses and wines as family after family passed through customs. We also lost a nice Austrian salami which was to be a present for my father. Eventually our visas, passports, and luggage were duly checked. We were allowed to proceed to the train station for a two day ride to our final destination, Montreal. I remember very little of that train trip except that the train was slow, noisy, and painted a dull colour. As the train at long last pulled into Montreal station we were tense with expectation: we would see our father again after a whole year, and more importantly my brother and I would finally take possession of our very own room stuffed with toys. That evening the sky turned a brilliant red. It was a sunset the likes of which I'd never seen before. This sunset remains my first memory of Montreal.

The taxi conveyed us from the wharf to our new home on St. Hubert Street. We were to live in a three storey walk-up apartment containing all the "luxuries": central heating, hot and cold running water, our own bathroom, a kitchen with a refrigerator, and "real plastic curtains." I have a photograph of my mother posing in front of these plastic curtains. She sent the photo to her parents in Graz. On the back she had written, "These are *genuine plastic*." Beside the building stood a gasoline station; across the road, a used car lot. On the next street over, a brick edifice could be seen—a potato chip factory oozing out a thick and oily smell. I remember entering the apartment for the first time. It seemed so spacious. But once inside, my brother and I had a major disappointment. We found no roomful of toys. Just a single balloon for each of us and a promise that toys would come eventually. (That Christmas, we did indeed receive an electric train set.)

In the days that followed, we went sightseeing. It was a strange sensation. We couldn't understand what people were saying. Nobody wore *Lederhosen* or shorts and no one went barefoot. People wore long blue jeans and rubber-soled shoes. Sounds and smells and foods were as unfamiliar as the sights. We couldn't talk to anyone. Children did not play on the street. When they played it was in alleyways separating row upon row of apartment houses. In these alleyways clotheslines with washing stretched everywhere. We discovered a playground but noticed no one played soccer, even though the fields were perfect. Some weeks later when my brother and I began going there with a soccer ball no one ever came to play soccer with us.

The streets were enormous. They were at least three time the width of street back home. And there were cars everywhere and huge buses belching out diesel fumes. Horse drawn carts brought milk and ice blocks to people's doors. The street cars looked so different from those in Graz. Not only were they bigger but they only had a single electrical pole to the wire above, instead of the rounded pantograph we thought they were supposed to have. The streets were busy with a buzzing, electrically charged tension. Everyone seemed in a hurry and people scurried about like ants. No one, for instance, stopped for a two hour lunch break as they did in Graz. Everything was bigger, more spacious, and faster moving than what I had known before.

Within a few days, the novelty and excitement wore off. I was ready to go back home. I now wanted to tell my friends and grandparents what I had just seen. Here reality set in. We *had* to stay in this place. I felt stranded and started yearning to see my grandparents and friends. We became very homesick. Tears and recriminations often arose within the family. "Why did my parents have to do this?," "Wasn't it selfish?," "Why can't we go back home?" Stretches of days would pass when my parents would not speak to each other nor my brother and I to them. We sulked. We pouted. We grumbled. We hurt each other with our words and our silences.

Squabbles were resolved only to be renewed. Various diversions to cure homesickness were attempted. With other immigrants we went to beaches along the St. Lawrence River. But they were homesick too. We kept sightseeing. Somehow this simply heightened our alienation. The social life around us did not touch us; its reality seemed unreachable. We did not fit in. Our culture was different, our language was different, the foods we ate were different. On the one hand, I think we wanted to belong; on the other we really could not because it was too soon. We did not know then that personal adjustment takes a long time. "Fitting in" also means giving something up about oneself. It was still too early for us to give up anything. We were not yet ready. So we remained outsiders. "We are Austrians and not Canadians," we said.

Besides, there was no way for us to return home. My parents had enough money to come to Montreal, but not to return. So we had to hold on, to persevere while my parents saved what money they could. (How often I heard the word "persevere" in those days!) My mother, who had completed her professional school diploma in Graz, found work first as a hot dog wrapper at Hygrade Meats, and subsequently in a small business gluing vinyl to the outside of boxes for record playing machines. I suspect my parents earned very little and after weekly bills were paid I doubt there was much money left over. But at least we had the hope that we would go back as soon as we could, instead of having to wait for five years.

During those first few weeks by brother and I were afraid to leave the apartment on our own. We watched for hours the flow of traffic from our first floor window overlooking St. Hubert Street. We learned the names of automobiles and made up games like counting how many Nashes, DeSotos or Chevrolets passed within a given time, or from how far away we could tell the car's make. In time, we also discussed the kind of car each of us would own once we grew up. He wanted a Cadillac. I liked Oldsmobiles.

My brother and I took our first independent steps to the corner service station where the owner spoke a little German. He let us wash windshields of cars being filled with gasoline. For this we sometimes got tips. The few cents we earned we immediately spent on something to which we took a keen liking: we bought Coca-Cola and cashew nuts from the dispensing machines. These machines ate up all our money.

In September, we enroled in school. Being totally ignorant of all aspects of the English language, I was placed again in grade 3. I recall vividly my first few weeks at Delorimier Elementary School. During recess I used to cower close to the brick walls of the school in the hope no one would notice me. From there I watched other boys at play. I didn't know their games nor could I ask anyone. At the time, baseball meant nothing to me. Neither did football, which was played with an oblong shaped air bag (we called it the *"Watchul"*) I thought did not even deserve to be called a "ball." Since I couldn't play games, I just stayed in the background; on the outside. From there I watched and watched.

Gradually patterns and meaning in behaviours became evident in what I saw. After endless repetition, English words and expressions, which at first sounded foreign, took on familiarity. Even baseball started to make sense. So did football. And that winter there was hockey, to which my brother and I took like fish to water even though neither of us knew how to skate. With our growing language skills, friendships with children our age developed. Our English and French speaking competence grew rapidly. The teachers at Delorimier school were generous and helpful. I owe them a monumental thank you. They gave up many of their lunches and after-school hours to teach my brother and me English. Each one of them encouraged and supported us. The vestiges of our Austrian accents took much longer to remove. For some time, we received considerable taunting from other children about being "German." No one in Canada distinguished between Austria and Germany. In the public mind of 1953, everyone who spoke German *was* German; furthermore they automatically were Nazis. Many children asked us whether we had personally known Adolf Hitler. We also received a lot of derision and "Heil Hitlers" until our German accents diminished.

Few Canadians actually seemed to know where Austria was. Some of our letters home to Oma and Opa took more than six weeks to reach them. We discovered that the Canadian Post Office was sending the letters by way of Australia. Postal workers obviously thought "AUSTRIA" was a misspelling of "AUSTRALIA." The Australians routed the mail back to where it should have gone in the first place. We solved this by writing in large block letters "EUROPE." on the envelopes to indicate to postal workers where Austria lay geographically, so to speak.

Blending into a new culture is a lot quicker and easier for children than for adults. My brother and I soon made new friendships with Canadian children because we were with them all day in school and we played together after school. My parents worked mainly with other Europeans who had Europeans values. Often they spoke German on the job, so learning English was not as easy for them. Our family also met frequently with other Austrian families. Austria always remained the standard of comparison. This new country was often found lacking. It had no opera houses, no visible culture, no concert music, no ski hills, no qualified tradespeople. With regard to the latter, anyone could seemingly pass himself off a an expert on just about anything. Everyday life seemed chaotic, fast-paced, materialistic, and opportunistic.

Particularly in business, one had to be on one's guard. Entrepreneurs took advantage of gullible immigrants. For instance, my father paid for a new television that was not delivered for many weeks; we bought clothing which fell apart after the first washing. Will I ever forget those used automobiles that left us stranded time and again due to their mechanical unfitness? Immigrants were vulnerable because, wanting to be accepted, they tended to trust and believe what they heard. Being ignorant of the legal system and non-proficient in English, they were easy targets. They were powerless to assert themselves and incapable of righting the wrongs committed against them.

For my brother and me, Canada gradually started to feel like home. We made friends, we learned English and could now speak it without difficulty. As with other Quebec boys, the hockey players of the Montreal Canadians became our idols. In small measures we forgot more and more of the written German language and the Austrian culture. There was no one except my parents with whom to practice the language, and even their German showed increasing sprinkles of English idioms and vocabulary. Changes were slowly taking place in ourselves. It was even alright to put one's feet onto the coffee table at home. We left Montreal two years after we arrived; not to go home but to take up residence in the Eastern Townships of Quebec. This was a new environment much closer to nature and to small town friendships than Montreal. There I spent three exceedingly happy years and made congenial Canadian friends.

The first five years in Canada passed quickly. My parents debated whether or not to return to Graz as planned. By then, my brother and I certainly did *not* want to go back. Our grandparents were already a somewhat distant memory having been supplanted by new-found friends. My parents themselves were unsure, but eventually they decided that we should return. My mother especially wanted to see her parents again. So in November of 1958, (I was 14 years old) my mother, my brother and I returned to Austria. My father stayed behind. He planned to work in Canada for at least another year before returning.

We took leave of our Canadian friends and travelled again by boat, this time from Montreal to Le Havre, and from there by train via Paris to Graz. Our homecoming provided us with a rude shock. The Graz to which we returned was a foreign city. It was so different from how I remembered it. Ironically, now that I was back, I felt I did not belong. My grandparents and former friends, although very kind and encouraging, seemed distant to me. The relatives felt more like strangers. All of them had grown older and no longer looked as I remembered them. My childhood friends had not put their lives on hold either awaiting my return; some I had difficulty recognizing; others I did not even remember. They had all carried on with their lives by forming new friendship circles to which I did not belong. What's more, I had difficulty speaking to them because expressing myself in the German language was difficult; it felt unnatural. Graz had also changed visually. The ruins in which I used to play six years before had disappeared. Unfamiliar new buildings stood in their places. New automobiles and mopeds raced about where I remembered only bicycles, old trucks, and horse-drawn carts.

My brother and I had to attend school. It lasted only two days. Our manners were all wrong. We offended teachers by not standing up when they addressed us. We intended no disrespect. However, we had not made such formal behaviour habitual in Canada and kept forgetting to stand up. I felt freakish as other boys made fun of my manners (or lack thereof) and ridiculed my broken German. The experience was so devastating my brother and I hated it and refused to return to the school. Both of us stubbornly clung to our demand to return to Canada. Homesickness had taken hold once again but this time in the other direction—we sought the community we left behind in the Eastern Townships of Quebec. All the pleading, all the promises, all the begging and convincing by my relatives fell on deaf ears. My brother and I sobbed at the thought of staying in Graz; we vehemently argued our own view and rebutted every other. We were stubborn and unrelenting in our insistence to leave. Seven weeks later our mother and the relatives gave in. It was decided we would return to Canada. Ironically enough, my grandparents made it possible for us to buy the tickets. From their savings they paid for the tickets with which we left them again. Not until I became an adult did I understand how deeply they must have cared for us to give up their own happiness for ours.

So there we were. We went through another round of farewells with grandparents and friends. But this time there was not the accompanying fear of the unknown because we at least knew where and to what we were going. The year was 1958. I was a 14 year old adolescent quickly approaching puberty. My friends and peer group were far more important than my family. But after our return to Canada, stability was brief. Within a year of returning, we relocated yet again. This time to Toronto.

Upon moving to Toronto I must say my life changed for the worse. I became truly disconsolate. Could there never be a home, a stable community or lasting friendships? Would I always be transplanted? Never able to grow roots? I felt hollow as if the ground had been moved from under me. I lost all interest in the new surroundings and could not seem to connect with anyone. I longed for old friends from the baseball and the hockey teams. I longed for my girlfriend. I had just experienced for the first time the sensation of being in love. This feeling brought a whole new dimension to relationships. I'm sure you know how special this feeling is. Having to leave her and my friendship group was very, very difficult, very hard.

Separated again from people and places for which I cared left me unattached and drifting. I became morose and introspective. I felt sorry for myself. I rejected everything my parents stood for including their Austrian heritage. The new school in Toronto was misery: a factory for some 2,500 students in which no part of the learner was brought to life. School consisted of passivity and memorization. I had never experienced academic difficulties in school but now my grades tumbled. Caught up in a situation of despair I felt crushed. It was 1959. I was 15 years old, and felt powerless to change my situation.

More than anything else, what carried me through those difficult high school years was the piano; notably the works of Mozart, Chopin, and especially Bach. Rather than seeking out people I immersed myself in music. On the piano my mind would drift into a fantasy world of old friends and familiar places. Within that world of music I could roam free, able to express feelings and engage in imaginary dialogues. Through music I also learned about composers and their not infrequent hardships. The piano became a very good friend. It was the first to point me in the direction where I would eventually find roots—the roots I was so desperately needing.

Most adolescents typically feel alienated from their parents and struggle against them for their freedom. I don't know whether my rejection of parental values during adolescent years owes its origin to my parents' taking the family out of Austria and moving us like migrants from place to place in Canada, or simply to the natural process of growing up. At any rate, frequent moving about and continual severing of social ties unfortunately left me without any community with which to connect.

Once high school finished I enroled in university to study philosophy and thereby entered a very dark period of my development. Psychological aberrations appeared. I can't explain why they happened but it had something to do with looking for a personal identity and security. Quite suddenly one morning I could not get out of bed for dizziness and nausea. I was bedridden for two weeks. Other unexplainable and uncontrollable *fears* subsequently sprang up. I did not know why I felt fear or of what I was afraid. I felt vulnerable; alone; abandoned; with nothing to cling to— no person, no beliefs, no values, no culture, no roots. Whenever I was with people in an enclosure, a panic to escape, claustrophobia, took hold. All the physical symptoms of panic accompanied these feelings: cold clammy hands, rapid breathing, racing heartbeat. It was as if another being had entered my body and played with it at will. My feelings were radically out of step with my conscious life. I felt lost and began to get deeply depressed. Like the fear of crowds, depressions were new and incomprehensible. Depressions came and went of their own accord and seemed to wash over me in waves. On one or two such occasions a horrible emptiness overtook me. My body felt like a vessel being drained of all its energy and life; gushing out its innermost core, leaving only a hollow shell. These sensations were exhausting. Despite all my conscious efforts to resist, something within myself kept tugging me toward a frightening, infinite nothingness. I underwent two years of group counselling. This did not relieve the symptoms but I could see that many others suffered from similar or more severe disorders. Further, I learned that such disorders were relatively common among young adults like me. One philosophy professor in whom I confided actually went so far as to tell me I was fortunate to have these experiences. He thought I would become stronger for going through them. I remember thinking that I have to undergo them successfully first—a proposition not to be taken for granted. On two occasions I came close to ending it all.

During the time I went to university my parents moved away from Toronto to another city. I was now on my own. After graduating with a B.A. in philosophy in 1967, I found a position in a high school as a teacher of English and German. Along with it came a personal and a professional awakening which brought a clear sense of direction. Dark introspection receded, giving way to hope. A positive inner reconstruction of myself gained in strength. The psychological aberrations I had experienced vanished as suddenly as they had appeared five years earlier. In 1969, at age 24, I felt the need to reconnect with my past. For the first time I returned to Europe on my own and there rekindled ties with my Austrian heritage; with the mountains, with my grandparents, with Graz, and with by best friend from childhood. My life became easier from then on. In time I married and together with my wife have raised a family which we intentionally have never moved.

At some point in their lives, most people ask themselves fundamental philosophical questions: "Does one's being have meaning and purpose?," "How does one fit into the scheme of things?," "Is there a higher world than the everyday world?" These are not questions asked only by immigrants although the search for answers is perhaps more urgent and intense for immigrants. On the one hand, immigrants are physically cut adrift from traditional answers given in their original cultures; on the other they never fully assimilate the answers given in the values of the new culture. So immigrants are left to their own resources to cobble together answers as best they can.

I have reflected often on how the difficult early years brought on my immigration have shaped my own life *positively*. In a sense much of what I have done since coming to Canada focused on constructing a home.

Music, the study of philosophy, questions about learning and education, all involve a personal search for meaning. For a long time (well into my early twenties) I felt no connection to any place; I had no sense of belonging anywhere. I made few friends because I feared the pain of losing them. It took many years to subdue these fears and to reconnect. I discovered that a home need not have its foundation in a single location, a single culture, or a single language. Immigration pushed me to construct my home in a mental-spiritual rather than in an exclusively physical domain. I now feel immensely happy and secure. So many good things have come my way. My former philosophy professor was right.

A few weeks ago, I heard a First Nation elder passing on this advice to young native people: "Never forget who you are; never forget where you come from; and you will never get lost." For a long time I did not know who I was. I didn't know where I belonged. I felt lost. I have long since learned that my Austrian heritage is an inerasable part of me and that a deep portion of my personality is and will remain European. My grandparents' graves are in the central cemetary of Graz and I need to visit them from time to time. I need to reassure myself that my home town of Graz still exists. Periodically, I need to relive those early memories: to climb the Austrian hills and think about my ancestors: where they lived and what their way of life was like. Then I reaffirm where I come from. I can get in touch with a part of myself and give it legitimacy.

We immigrants are really very, very fortunate. We are bridge builders. We construct spans that join cultures. We are uniquely able to link lifestyles in a way that benefits both our old and new homes. The new country and its culture never replace the old. Instead, the best of the old and the best of the new are integrated. In the process both cultures are enriched, gradually transformed, and revitalized. I look forward to new initiatives between Canada and Austria and stand ready to participate fully in this bridging process.